SUCCESSFUL BIBLE TEACHING

A CREATIVE APPROACH

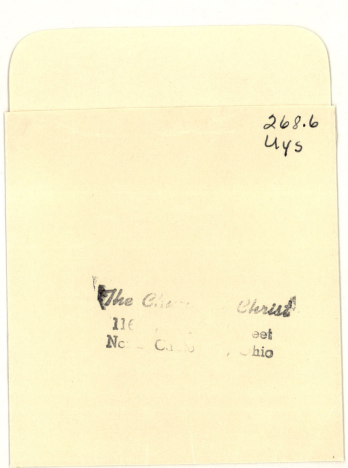

SUCCESSFUL BIBLE TEACHING

A CREATIVE APPROACH

SUE UYS

BAKER BOOK HOUSE
GRAND RAPIDS, MICHIGAN

Special thanks to
Becky Tilotta for the diagram on page 43 and the basic idea for "What Is Heaven Like?" on page 36.

Lady Collings for the use of the figure drawings on pages 38-41.

Standard Publishing Company for the use of the puppet stand idea on page 60.

Jay Bordine for the photographs on pages 58, 59, 67.

Carol Bruce and Joy Starkey for editing the manuscript.

Anyone who may have originated some of the ideas developed in this book.

Quotations from *The New English Bible* © the Delegates of the Oxford University Press, and the Syndics of the Cambridge University Press 1961, 1970 are used with permission of Oxford University Press.

Copyright © 1973 by
Baker Book House Company

ISBN: 0-8010-9200-0

Printed in the United States of America

This book is dedicated to
the students of my first two teacher-training classes—
those ladies of the church of Christ
in East London, South Africa,
whose enthusiastic response
inspired me to prepare
the course for publication.

FOREWORD

This book is designed primarily for Christians who wish to learn to teach preschool (ages 2 to 5), primary (grades 1-3), and junior (grades 4-6) children's Bible classes. It is a foundation on which a teacher can build for the rest of his or her career.

The book will also be of special interest to experienced teachers and missionaries, at home and abroad, who feel the need to train prospective teachers. In many churches, teachers are weary and in need of a rest from teaching; but there are no new teachers to replace them. At the back of the book are some suggestions for conducting a teacher-training class, using this book as a basis.

Christian mothers, too, will find the book helpful. Teaching Scripture to her children in the home is a Christian mother's greatest privilege and responsibility.

CONTENTS

PART ONE
SOMETHING TO HEAR

1 A Brief Review of the Bible's Contents 17
2 Reading the Bible and Taking Useful Notes 20

PART TWO
SOMETHING TO SEE

3 Collecting Materials for Making Visual Aids 31
4 Flip Charts 34
5 Flannelgraph 42
6 Puppets 55
7 Models 66
8 Decorating the Classroom to Emphasize a Theme 85

PART THREE
SOMETHING TO DO

9 Story-Centered Class Activities 95
10 Helping Children Apply the Principles of Bible
   Stories 105

PART FOUR
AN ORGANIZED TEACHER

11 Lesson Plans 119
12 Filing Teaching Materials 126
13 A Teacher's Total Preparation 130

   Bibliography 142

INTRODUCTION
THE TEACHER'S CHALLENGE

"Thy word is a lamp unto my feet, and a light unto my path" (Ps. 119:105). When David wrote these words, he understood clearly the need for God's guidance in his life. Trying to make it on his own, he had sinned and suffered wretchedly.

One would have no need of a light along a pathway unless there were darkness and danger there. Each child must take the pathway of life, and he will find both the darkness of sin and the dangers of temptation along that path. God's Word is a light because it shows us what sin is and how it can destroy us. It teaches us that He created us and loves us dearly, and it sets forth the best way to walk if we are to be happy now and live eternally.

But a light can be of no value unless it is turned on. "Turning it on" in this context will mean teaching it. Our challenge will be to teach God's Word effectively, that we may prevent many children from ruining their lives with sin.

If one did nothing more than open the Bible and read it to a group of children, they would learn something. But those who teach children in public schools as well as Bible schools have found that reading is not enough. Children learn their lessons much more effectively when they can *see* pictures and objects that illustrate what they read and *hear*. They also remember better when they *do* things that relate to their lessons.

If we study and use good teaching principles and methods to teach God's perfect Word, we cannot help but succeed in reaching our goal. For God has said, "My word . . . shall not return unto me void, but it shall accomplish that which I please, and it shall prosper in the thing whereto I sent it" (Isa. 55:11).

WHAT THIS BOOK CAN TEACH YOU

- ☐ How to understand the contents of the Bible better
- ☐ How to read the Bible and make useful teaching notes
- ☐ How to organize Bible stories into groups for teaching
- ☐ How to choose appropriate subject material for different age groups
- ☐ What materials you can start collecting for making visual aids
- ☐ Four methods of teaching with visual aids that will enable you to teach any story in the Bible
- ☐ What basic equipment you will need and how to make it
- ☐ How to prepare and teach stories using each method
- ☐ How to use visual aids with older children
- ☐ How to decorate the classroom to help emphasize the theme of the group of stories you are teaching
- ☐ How to apply the principles of Bible stories to life today
- ☐ Some good classroom activities that will help children remember what they learn
- ☐ Six different ways children can make pictures in class
- ☐ How to write good lesson plans to help your class period run smoothly
- ☐ How to file your teaching materials
- ☐ How to teach more effectively with quarterlies

PART ONE

SOMETHING TO HEAR

1

A BRIEF REVIEW OF THE BIBLE'S CONTENTS

Do you have an overall view of the subject you are going to teach? Let's establish one for you. It will help you understand the structure into which all Bible stories are fitted.

THE CENTRAL THEME OF THE BIBLE

One scholar has suggested that there is a silver thread running through the Bible. Watch for it. *Someone is coming. . . . Someone came. . . . Someone is coming again.* That someone, of course, is Christ. The significance of the whole Bible lies in the fact that Christ came to earth, giving all of us the hope of overcoming sin now and eternally.

TWO GENERAL TYPES OF BIBLE LITERATURE

As you read through the Bible you will find two general types of material: historical and doctrinal. The historical stories depict activities through which God worked among people to bring about His plans to save mankind from sin. These stories usually have morals or lessons we can learn from their characters, in addition to gaining historical knowledge. The doctrinal material includes instruction for living a happy, useful Christian life, along with symbolic descriptions of the Christian's relationship with spiritual things such as God, Christ, heaven, the church, and so forth. Notice that doctrinal passages are usually instructions or descriptions, rather than stories. However, throughout this course we will call any passage of Scripture a Bible story when it is used as the basis for a Bible lesson.

THE ORDER OF BIBLE BOOKS

As you may already know, the books of the Bible are not in historical or chronological order. The sixty-six books are grouped according to the specific type of material they contain:

Old Testament

Law	Genesis–Deuteronomy
History	Joshua–Esther
Poetry	Job–Song of Solomon
Prophecy	Isaiah–Malachi

New Testament

The Gospels	Matthew–John
History	Acts
Letters	Romans–Jude
Prophecy	Revelation

PERIODS OF BIBLE HISTORY

All the books of the Bible were written about or during one of the following periods of history. These periods are listed in the order in which they occurred.

1. **Antediluvian Period:** the period before the Flood. God creates man a free moral agent. Man severs himself from God by choosing evil. God plans to destroy the earth by a flood.

2. **Postdiluvian Period:** the period after the Flood.

3. **Patriarchal Period:** God speaks to the people through the fathers of the households. In this period we learn of the beginning of the Israelite nation, through which Christ would be born. The rest of the Old Testament is a history of the development of this nation.

4. **Egyptian Bondage:** the children of Israel become slaves in Egypt.

5. **Wilderness Wanderings:** the children of Israel wander in the desert after leaving Egypt. God gives them the Ten Commandments and numerous other instructions for worshiping Him and preserving themselves physically and spiritually.

6. **The Conquest of Canaan:** the Israelites enter the Promised Land.

7. **Judges:** the children of Israel are given judges to rule over them.

8. **United Kingdom:** the children of Israel are given their first king. Three kings rule during this period—Saul, David, and Solomon.

9. **The Divided Kingdom:** the Israelites split into two nations—Judah and Israel. This period lasts until Israel is taken captive by Assyria.

10. **Judah Alone:** Judah continues to stand as a nation.

11. **Babylonian Captivity:** Judah falls captive to Babylon.

12. **Restoration Period:** Ezra, Nehemiah, and others lead in rebuilding Jerusalem. The Jews attempt to become a nation again.

13. **Period Between the Old and New Testaments.**

14. **The Life, Ministry, and Death of Christ.**

15. **The Establishment, Development, and Growth of the Church.**

2

READING THE BIBLE AND TAKING USEFUL NOTES

Have you read through your Bible completely? Now is a good time to begin if you haven't done it. You will be able to teach parts of the Bible much more effectively when you have read the whole. For instance, when you are teaching a particular story from the Old Testament, you will know the incidents that precede and follow it. This may help you to explain something in the story you are teaching. Also, you will be able to give examples of other stories that teach the same moral or lesson. In this chapter we want to present a plan for daily Bible reading and note taking.

MATERIALS YOU WILL NEED

A Bible—preferably one of the newer versions written in today's English.

A package of 3" x 5" cards.

READING THE BIBLE IN CHRONOLOGICAL ORDER

Instead of reading through the Bible in its present order, let's read it in its chronological order; that is, putting the books into their place in Bible history and reading them that way. In a small tract, *Through the Bible in a Year,* Leslie B. Flynn has arranged them for us. He has inserted the books of poetry and prophecy from the Old Testament into the historical books at about the time they are thought to have been written. In the same way, the epistles or letters of the New Testament are inserted into the narrative of the Book of Acts. (The periods of history are not listed in this tract.) You will enjoy reading the Bible in this order and will probably find the books more meaningful to you.

The amount you read each day is up to you. If you would like to try to complete the Bible in a year, you will need to read about three chapters a day.

Here is the listing:

1. **Antediluvian Period**
   Genesis 1—5

2. **Postdiluvian Period**
   Genesis 6—11

3. **Patriarchal Period**
   Genesis 12—50
   Job

4. **Egyptian Bondage**
   Exodus 1—12

5. **Wilderness Wanderings**
   Exodus 13—40
   Leviticus
   Numbers
   Deuteronomy

6. **Conquest of Canaan**
   Joshua

7. **Judges**
   Judges
   Ruth

8. **United Kingdom**
   I Samuel
   II Samuel
   Psalms
   I Kings 1—4
   Proverbs
   Ecclesiastes
   Song of Solomon
   I Kings 5—11

9. **Divided Kingdom**
   I Kings 12—22

II Kings 1—14:20
Joel
II Kings 14:21-25
Jonah
II Kings 14:26-29
Amos
II Kings 15—17

10. **Judah Alone**

    Hosea
    II Kings 18—19
    Isaiah
    Micah
    Nahum
    II Kings 20—21
    Zephaniah
    Habakkuk
    II Kings 22—25

11. **Babylonian Captivity**

    Obadiah
    Jeremiah
    Lamentations
    I Chronicles
    II Chronicles
    Ezekiel
    Daniel

12. **Restoration Period**

    Esther
    Ezra 1—4
    Haggai
    Zechariah
    Ezra 5—10
    Nehemiah
    Malachi

13. **Period Between the Old and New Testaments**

14. **Life, Ministry, and Death of Christ**

    Matthew
    Mark
    Luke
    John

15. **Establishment, Development, and Growth of the Church**

    Acts 1—14
    James
    Galatians
    Acts 15—18:11
    I Thessalonians
    II Thessalonians
    Acts 18:12—19:10
    I Corinthians
    Acts 19:11—20:1
    II Corinthians
    Acts 20:2
    Romans
    Acts 20:3—28
    Ephesians
    Philippians
    Colossians
    Hebrews
    Philemon
    I Peter
    II Peter
    I Timothy
    Titus
    II Timothy
    I John
    II John
    III John
    Jude
    Revelation

KEEPING A CARD FILE ON "TEACHABLE" STORIES

Not all of what you read in the Bible is suitable for teaching children. We need to teach things that will be meaningful to them. For example, children would benefit very little from much of the teaching on the law in the first few books of the Bible. *Egermeier's Bible Story Book,* by Elsie E. Egermeier, contains, in simple language, over three hundred stories that are suitable for children. You might like to buy a copy of this book to help you in selecting and simplifying stories.

It will be most helpful to you later if you record some facts as you read through your Bible. Make out a 3" x 5" card for each story or text. On the card, write or type the headings you see on the sample.

```
Title:

Scripture:

Period of History:

Moral or Subject:

Methods:

Summary:
```

You should be able to fill out the first three sections of the card without any difficulty. On the next page is a list of morals and subjects that will help you understand what you are to record under the fourth heading. (Sometimes you will find more than one possible theme.) When you have completed the five chapters on visual aids, you will be able to go back and fill in the information under "Methods." You can either fill in the type of visual aid you think would be good for each story, or record a visualized story you have prepared or bought. If you have already read through your Bible on another plan, you may not want to make summaries of the stories. The purpose of this part of your note taking is to help you remember the contents of each story.

Notice the information you might fill in on the stories from the Antediluvian Period:

Title: God Made the World

Scripture: Genesis 1 and 2

Period of History: Antediluvian

Moral or Subject: God's Greatness

Methods: Magazine Picture Flip Chart

Summary:

Title: Adam and Eve Disobey God

Scripture: Genesis 3

Period: Antediluvian

Moral or Subject: Disobedience, The Devil, or perhaps Pride

Methods: TEV Flip Chart

Summary:

Title: The First Children

Scripture: Genesis 4:1-16, 25-26

Period: Antediluvian

Moral or Subject: Jealousy, Anger, or Improper Worship

Methods: Homemade Flannelgraph

Summary:

When you are reading the Gospels you might make a card for each story in Matthew. Then as you go through the other three Gospels, instead of making new cards for stories that are repeated, go back and fill in the additional references on the cards from Matthew. Do the same for stories recorded for the first time in the other Gospels. Then when you are telling a story from one of the Gospels, you can incorporate the information that appears in the others.

I would suggest that you take your pack of cards and write the six headings on all of them first. Then, as you read, simply jot down the information under each heading. This will speed up your reading program. File the cards in a small box (a recipe box is perfect) or put an elastic band around them. File stories in their Biblical rather than chronological order, so you will be able to find them easily. As the course proceeds, you will see the great advantage of having a card file such as this!

GROUPING STORIES IN SERIES OR UNITS

Children learn and remember better when stories they hear over a period of time are related to one another. Groups of related stories are called series or units. The main idea of a unit is called the theme. In Bible school, a unit can be as short as five or six lessons and is not usually longer than thirteen lessons, covering one-quarter of a year. There are three good ways to group Bible stories to teach in this way:

By Periods of History. This is a series of stories that follow one after another in the order that they occurred in history. For example, you might teach a series from the period of the judges, or any of the other periods of history given in chapter 1.

By Morals. As your card file expands you will notice that many stories project identical morals or lessons, such as the importance of obedience. Morals of stories usually consist of good or bad behavior patterns or attitudes. Here is a list of some of the morals you will find repeatedly in Bible stories:

Trusting God	Anger
Love	Patience
Thankfulness	Compassion
Kindness	Courage
Giving	Working
Doing good to others	Laziness
Honesty	Pride
Lying	Humility
Cheating	Selfishness
Greed	Sacrificing
Hatred	Studying
Jealousy	Witnessing

By Subjects. In a series like this, you might teach all the stories that show different aspects of the same subject, such as worship. Other subjects you could use as themes are:

God's love	God's greatness
God's patience	God's blessings
God's wisdom	God's loving care

The creation
Children of the Bible
Jesus, our Shepherd
The miracles of Jesus
The parables of Jesus
The Sermon on the Mount
The Beatitudes
Heaven
The apostles
The devil
Christ, our Savior
Christ, our example
Conversion
Forgiveness
Repentance
The Church—God's family
The Christian
Preaching the gospel in all the world

USING QUARTERLIES AS UNIT OUTLINES

Quarterlies are invaluable aids when it comes to selecting themes and Bible stories that teach them. They contain thirteen related stories or passages of Scripture with instructions for teaching them to specific age groups. Common age group divisions are as follows: preschool, ages 2—5 (this group is usually broken down into 2's and 3's in one class and 4's and 5's in another); primary, grades 1—3; and junior, grades 4—6.

If you are going to teach in an established congregation with a religious educational director, you will likely be given quarterlies from which to teach. However, in many situations, teachers need to know how to make up their own units. Here is some information that will help you further toward this end.

CHOOSING APPROPRIATE THEMES FOR VARIOUS AGE GROUPS

Preschool children have very little concept of time. Therefore, units based on long periods of history are not very suitable for them. However, you can take any outstanding Bible characters from the periods and teach units on their lives. For example, the life of Jesus, Abraham, or Joseph.

Small children need to develop a positive outlook toward God and His Word. From the list of subjects, you might choose themes from numbers 1—10. Numbers 1—6 from the list of morals are also suitable themes for preschoolers.

Primary children can learn the main stories from any of the periods of history. However, units based on good and bad attitudes and behavior such as numbers 7—21 under "Morals" might be more beneficial to them. Subject numbers 11—16 are also good themes for primary children.

Junior children begin learning history and geography in school. This is the best time to teach children Bible history units. Units based on heroes in any of these periods will also be of special interest to juniors.

Subjects that relate to salvation and the church can be taught to juniors. Notice numbers 17—25 from the list of subjects.

In the listings of these themes and the suggestions for using them with children of different ages, there is considerable overlapping. These are only suggestions to help you decide appropriate themes if you need to make up your own units. Also, if you know these things ahead of time, you will have a better idea of what to look for in the Bible as you are reading it. We will discuss unit planning further in chapter 11.

Whether you are going to outline your own units or use those given in quarterlies, you will want to present the stories to the children in the most interesting way you can. We are now ready to study and experiment with some exciting ways to share Bible stories with children. As you prepare the stories in the next section, tell them to children around your home. Their interest and enthusiasm will inspire you.

PART TWO

SOMETHING TO SEE

3

COLLECTING MATERIALS FOR MAKING VISUAL AIDS

Visual aids are those things we use in telling Bible stories, to help children see how things looked at that period or what they meant. There is much good visual aid material on the market today. You can go to your nearest religious bookstore and ask them for a catalog of things that are available. Also, you will find many good teaching aids in the children's toy department of any store.

But it is not necessary to buy all of your visual aids. In this chapter is a list of materials you can start collecting to make some good visual aids of your own. In addition to this list, there will be short lists in some of the following chapters. You will be able to find most work materials around the house or in the supply cupboard at your church building.

WORKING TOOLS

Pencil   Crayons
Pen   Magic markers (felt pens)
Ruler   Masking tape
Scissors   Stapler
Paper glue

All of these things will fit nicely into a large shoe box. To label the box, print "Tools" on a piece of masking tape with black magic marker and stick it on the box. It would be good to label in this manner all boxes in which you keep teaching materials. You will find it a great help. If you have a cupboard for your materials, you may not want to keep your working tools in a box as suggested. As with all filing suggestions we make, adjust them to your own particular situation whenever necessary.

PAPER

Shiny colored paper   Cardboard
Construction paper   Cardboard boxes
Wrapping paper   Cardboard cylinders from
Gummed colored paper   wax paper rolls, paper
Carbon paper   towels, bathroom tissue,
*Wall paper   etc.
Posterboard

*You can get obsolete wallpaper books from firms that sell wallpaper. Some charge a small fee, but it is worth it. Wallpapers in plain colors or small prints are most suitable.

SEWING SCRAPS

Material   Fur, leather, etc.
Buttons   Spools from thread
Wool   Embroidery thread
Felt

LETTERS

Letters cut from magazines　　　Stencils for drawing letters
Sheets of ready-to-stick letters　　Patterns for letters to cut out

PICTURES

You will need all the good pictures you can find. There are some types of pictures especially good for illustrating and making modern applications of Bible stories. Notice them in Section II of the Suggested Filing System on page 128. Look for pictures in the following and other sources:

> Magazines　　　　Calendars
> Coloring books　　Greeting cards
> Newspapers　　　Postcards
> Catalogs　　　　　Used quarterlies
> Old story books

It would be a good idea to make up the picture section of your filing system now. Read over the information "How to Prepare and Arrange File Folders" on page 129. Label a file folder for each type of picture listed in Section II. As you collect pictures, trim them neatly and file them in their proper folders.

In the next four chapters, you will learn how to tell Bible stories four different ways, using homemade visual aids. There will be sample stories for you to prepare using each method. It is not my purpose to show you many ways of making each type of visual aid. Rather, you will learn how to make or collect basic sets of materials from which you can quickly prepare to illustrate any story in the Bible.

> IMPORTANT: Whichever method you use to tell Bible stories, be sure you <u>always</u> teach with an open Bible on your table. Let the children know that each story they hear comes from God's Word.

4

FLIP CHARTS

Flip charts are homemade books. In this chapter we will learn how to make flip charts with two types of pictures: printed pictures and "elaborate stick figures."

MATERIALS YOU WILL NEED

Stiff paper, colored or plain
Your picture files described on page 33
Today's English Version of the New Testament (TEV) (also titled Good News for Modern Man)
Two unattached ring binders, or
A ring binder cover with two rings

HOW TO MAKE A FLIP CHART

Prepare a picture for each point in the story. Mount or draw the pictures on uniform sized sheets of stiff paper. (Don't make the sheets too small.)

Using letters from any source listed on page 33, make a title page for your booklet. It might include the title of the story in bold letters and the Scripture reference in smaller letters. If you like, put a picture somewhere on the page to illustrate what the booklet is going to be about.

If you are using loose rings, punch two holes, about three inches apart, in the top center of each page. Fasten the pages together with the rings.

Another alternative is this: Turn a two-ring binder cover inside out and use it as a holder for your story. It doesn't matter if your pages are larger than the cover. Punch holes in the pages of the story the same distance apart as the rings in the cover. Put the pages into the rings.

Write the section of the story each picture represents on the back of the preceding page. Therefore, on the back of your title page, write the section of story for your first picture, and so on.

HOW TO MAKE "ELABORATE STICK FIGURE" PICTURES

Do you have a copy of Today's English Version of the New Testament (*Good News for Modern Man*)? This is an inexpensive, modern version with simple pictures to illustrate many of the stories. These pictures are like stick figures, only more elaborate. If you look through the book, you will see the possibilities of illustrating numerous doctrinal or historical stories from either the Old or New Testament, using the pictures it contains. Although each picture represents a particular story, you can take the same picture and make it say what you want it to in another story.

The pictures are easy to copy. However, you will need to enlarge them considerably. If there is a point for which you can't find a picture, it is quite easy to draw one on the same style. If you find copying pictures difficult, there is an inexpensive machine (approximately eight dollars) called a Magnajector, which can be used to enlarge small pictures like these to the size you require.

If you color the clothing and significant details in these pictures, you will make them more interesting. Add color with crayons, colored markers, colored paper, and so forth. To do the latter, take your enlarged picture, and put a sheet of carbon paper behind it, the carbon side away from your picture back. Put a sheet of colored paper under the carbon paper. Now trace over the part of the picture you want to color in. Cut it out from the colored sheet and paste it in place on your picture. It is a good idea to outline your drawings with a thin black marker.

If you cannot obtain a copy of Today's English Version, draw regular stick figure pictures. Make them interesting in the same ways we have suggested for the TEV figures.

TIPS FOR TELLING FLIP CHART STORIES

1. If you are using a ring binder cover as your base or holder, hold the two sides of the cover together at the left side. Flip the pages one at a time with the right hand.

2. If your pages are fastened with loose rings, keep the hand that is holding the book moving toward the back of the book as you turn the pages, so that it doesn't cover up part of the picture you are showing.

3. As you show the children each picture, read the part of the story it represents from the back of the preceding page.

A STORY TO PREPARE
(using pictures from your picture file)

When you have collected pictures in your folders, you will be able to make up many flip charts. The pictures you are collecting are very good for illustrating doctrinal passages, such as the description of heaven in the story below. Make a flip chart for this story. Use pictures from your picture file to illustrate each of the fifteen points.

When possible, use colored pictures. If you use a black and white picture, make it colorful by drawing colored lines around it. Or, you might mount the picture on colored paper.

What is Heaven Like?
Revelation 21

1. Heaven is more beautiful than a bride ready for her husband.

2. It is more beautiful than a city made of gold and precious stones.

3. There will be no crying.

4. No one will ever die.

5. People will never grow old.
6. There will be no darkness.
7. There will be nothing to frighten us or make us unhappy.
8. No storms.
9. No fires.
10. No war.
11. No pain.
12. No sickness.
13. No accidents.
14. No starving.
15. In heaven everyone will be happy. I want to go there, don't you?

Other passages of Scripture you could illustrate beautifully with pictures from your files are these: "The Lord Is My Shepherd," Psalm 23; "Parables of the Kingdom," Matthew 13; and "The Sermon on the Mount," Matthew 5—7.

A STORY TO PREPARE
(using "elaborate stick figure" pictures)

Below is a doctrinal story, showing how God loves His children and wants them to do what is right and good for them. The TEV pictures for the story are at the end of the lesson. Make a flip chart for this story, enlarging and adding color to the pictures as we have already suggested. The page in the TEV from which the picture was copied is indicated on each frame. Those which have no page numbers have been improvised. Each frame is numbered to correspond with the part of the story it represents.

The Prodigal Son
Luke 15:11-32

1. A man had two sons. One day the youngest son said to his father, "Give me my share of your property." The father gave it to him; then he sold it to get some money.

2. He took his money and went away to a far country. There he wasted his money in reckless living. He spent everything he had!

3. Then a famine came over the country and he was left without a thing.

4. He went to live with one of the citizens in that country. The man put him to work feeding the pigs. He was so hungry he would have liked to eat the food the pigs were eating. He remembered his father's house and wished he were even as comfortable as his father's servants.

5. He decided to go back home and ask his father to make him a servant in the house. He didn't feel worthy to be his father's son anymore.

6. But when the father saw him coming home, he ran to meet him.

7. He threw his arms around him and hugged him. He was so glad to see his son again!

8. The son said, "Father, I am no longer worthy to be called your son. Let me be one of your servants."

9. But the father was so happy. He told his servants to bring a robe and shoes and a ring for his son.

10. He told them to kill a fat calf and prepare a great feast to celebrate.

11. The older son was returning from the field and heard the noise of the feasting and dancing. When he learned his brother was home and his father was treating him so well, he got very angry. He wouldn't even go into the house.

12. When the father came out to talk to him, the son said, "I have always worked hard for you and never disobeyed you. You have never given me even a goat to share with my friends in a feast. But this good-for-nothing son, who has treated you badly, comes home and you kill the best calf for him." The father explained that all he owned belonged now to his eldest son, but they should be happy that a lost son had come home.

THE PRODIGAL SON

Luke 15:11-32

Adapted from *Good News for Modern Man*, © 1971 by American Bible Society

2   Page 193

3   Page 194

4   Page 194

5   Drawn

FLIP CHARTS ■ 39

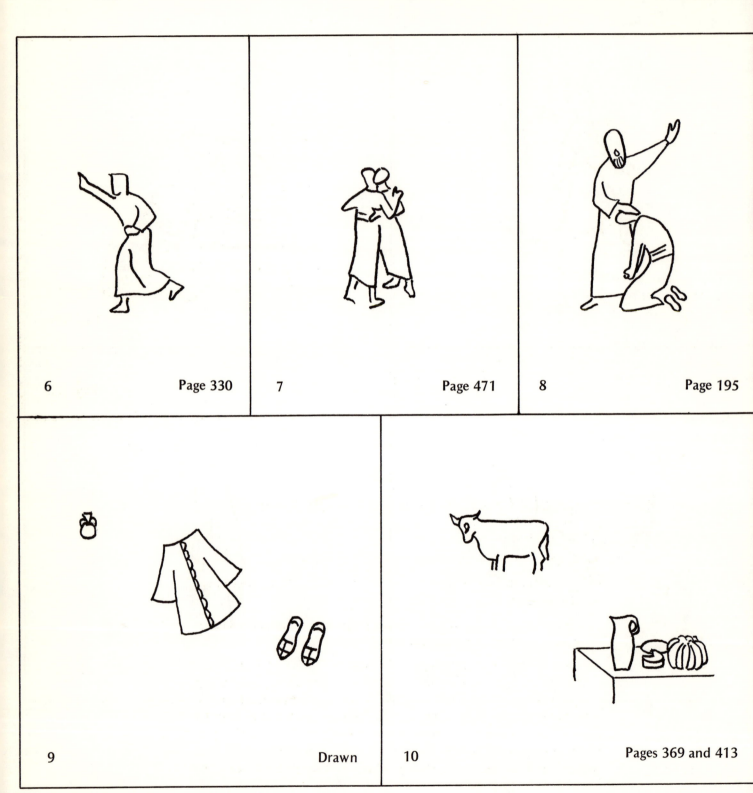

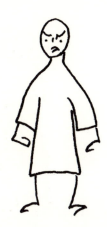

11   Drawn   12   Page 432

SUGGESTIONS FOR FILING FLIP CHART STORIES

1. Remove story from rings.

2. Tie pages together with string or plastic bag twisters.

3. Prepare a file folder. See Sections IV and V of the Suggested Filing System on page 128.

4. File Bible story flip charts and all flat prepared stories under Old or New Testament in their Biblical order.

5. As soon as you have prepared or bought an illustrated Bible story, prepare a card for it if you haven't already done so in your reading program. Under "Methods," record the one you have used. In the right-hand corner draw a red star. Do this for all the stories in the next three chapters, as well as any visualized Bible stories you make or buy in the future. Then when you are preparing a unit you will be able to see at a glance which stories you are ready to present with visual aids.

5

FLANNELGRAPH

Telling stories on the flannelboard is one of the oldest methods employed by Bible teachers of children. It is still an excellent method. Homemade flannelgraph stories are becoming very popular today. In this chapter we will discuss two types of homemade stories, as well as printed flannelgraph stories.

MATERIALS YOU WILL NEED

A flannelboard
A table easel
1 yard of pellon or vylene
Coloring and pattern books for tracing figures
Printed flannelgraph packets
Background scenes

HOW TO MAKE A FLANNELBOARD (DIAGRAM 1-A)

Cut a piece of stiff corrugated cardboard or lightweight plywood 24" x 36". Cover it with light blue or white flannel material. Tape or staple the material edges securely behind the board.

HOW TO MAKE A TABLE EASEL (DIAGRAM 1-B)

Cut away the bottom and top of a big cardboard box. Collapse it flat. On one corner draw half the pattern to the suggested measurements. Cut out the pattern through both thicknesses of cardboard, making a two-sided, folding easel. For a more sturdy easel, cut the pattern from plywood and fasten the two sides together with hinges.

DIAGRAM 1

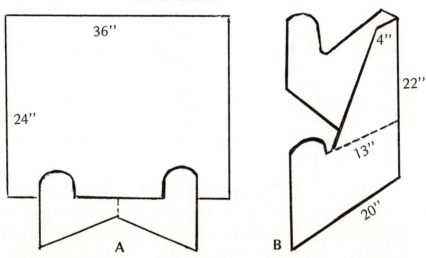

The two diagrams above are taken from the book *Your Handful of Ideas*, by Becky Tilotta. This book contains many useful ideas for teaching. The suggested measurements were not on the original diagrams.

HOW TO USE PRINTED FLANNELGRAPH PACKETS

There are many beautiful flannelgraph stories available. In them the characters and props are made to resemble the people and surroundings of Bible days. Therefore, they are good for telling historical stories. In a flannelgraph packet, you get a booklet of instructions for laying out all the figures needed to tell the story or stories included.

The booklet also shows easy background scenes you can draw and color with crayons. These make your stories even more realistic. You can draw background scenes on pieces of flannel a little larger than your board and lay them over your covered board as scenes change in the story.

In addition, you can make overlays to change the scenes without making new backgrounds. For example, to change a plain room to a prison cell, add a door and a window on which bars are drawn. Overlays can be made of felt or flannel.

HOW TO MAKE FIGURES FOR FLANNELGRAPH STORIES

Using homemade figures, you can tell any type of Bible or application story on the flannelboard. (We will discuss application stories in chapter 10.) You will find pattern and coloring books excellent sources of pictures for this purpose. Select the pictures you need to illustrate a story, then prepare figures for the flannelboard according to the instructions below.

There are some materials especially good for making flannelgraph figures. One of the best is lightweight vylene or pellon. This is the material used as interfacing in collars and other areas of a garment where stiffness is required. It sticks easily to flannel and is quite transparent for tracing through. Don't buy the iron-on kind.

To make figures from this material, draw or trace the objects you require onto the smooth side of the material. Outline the figures with black felt marker or crayon. Color them with crayon and cut them out. For good results with coloring in, rub your crayon back and forth firmly but evenly, going the same horizontal direction over the whole object. Then shade more heavily around the inside edges of the picture.

If you would like to prepare a story using silhouettes, cut the figures from black pellon or felt.

Figures cut from any kind of paper can also be made to stick to the flannelboard. Just stick bits of flannel, felt, sandpaper, or scraps of suede backed paper from flannelgraph packets, onto the back of the figures.

If you cannot obtain pellon for the two stories in this chapter, color the paper patterns and make them adhesive to flannel as we have suggested.

TIPS FOR TELLING FLANNELGRAPH STORIES

1. Have all backgrounds and figures ready and in order before you begin the story.

2. Know the story well enough to tell it, rather than read it.

3. Put up one figure on the board at a time, as you come to it in the story.

4. Smooth your hand across each figure to secure it firmly to the board.

A STORY TO PREPARE
(using homemade flannelgraph figures)

Below is a doctrinal story, describing the kingdom of heaven. For this story you will need a piece of net or mesh big enough to drape over your flannelboard, the fish drawn and colored from the patterns on pages 46–50, and a container to serve as a pail for the good fish. Here is the story as recorded in the *New English Bible*. In brackets are some instructions for telling it.

The Kingdom of Heaven Is Like a Fish Net
Matthew 13:47-50

"The kingdom of Heaven is like a net let down into the sea [spread your net across the board], where fish of every kind were caught in it. [Lift the net up and put the fish on the board, one at a time. As you do so, say the names of the fish as examples.] When it was full, it was dragged ashore. Then the men sat down and collected the good fish into pails and threw the worthless away. [Take the fish down from the board one at a time. Put the salmon, cod, tuna, and chad into a container marked "good fish." Lay the others aside as if to discard them.]

"This is how it will be at the end of time. The angels will go forth, and they will separate the wicked from the good, and throw them into the blazing furnace, the place of wailing and grinding of teeth." (NEB)

You can teach any number of parables on the flannelboard. Other lessons you might also teach are: "The Creation," Genesis 1; "Noah and the Ark," Genesis 6–9; teachings from Proverbs such as "The Little Creatures," Proverbs 30:24-28; "The Ten Plagues," Exodus 7–12; and "The Lord's Prayer," Matthew 6:9-15.

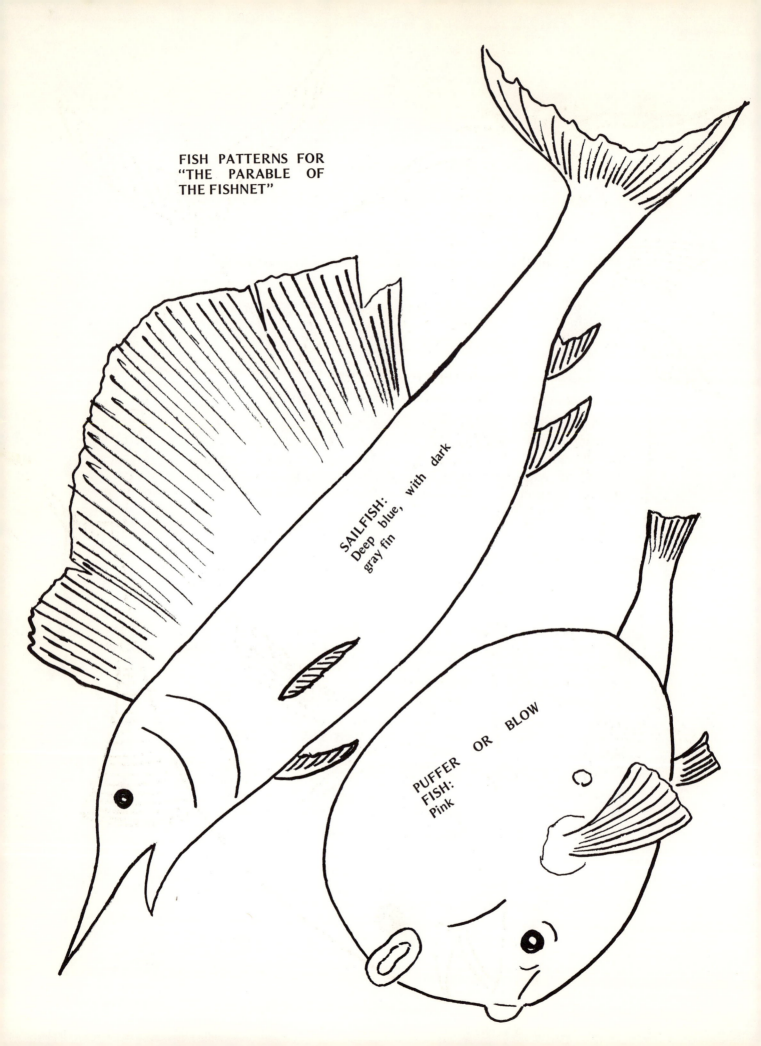

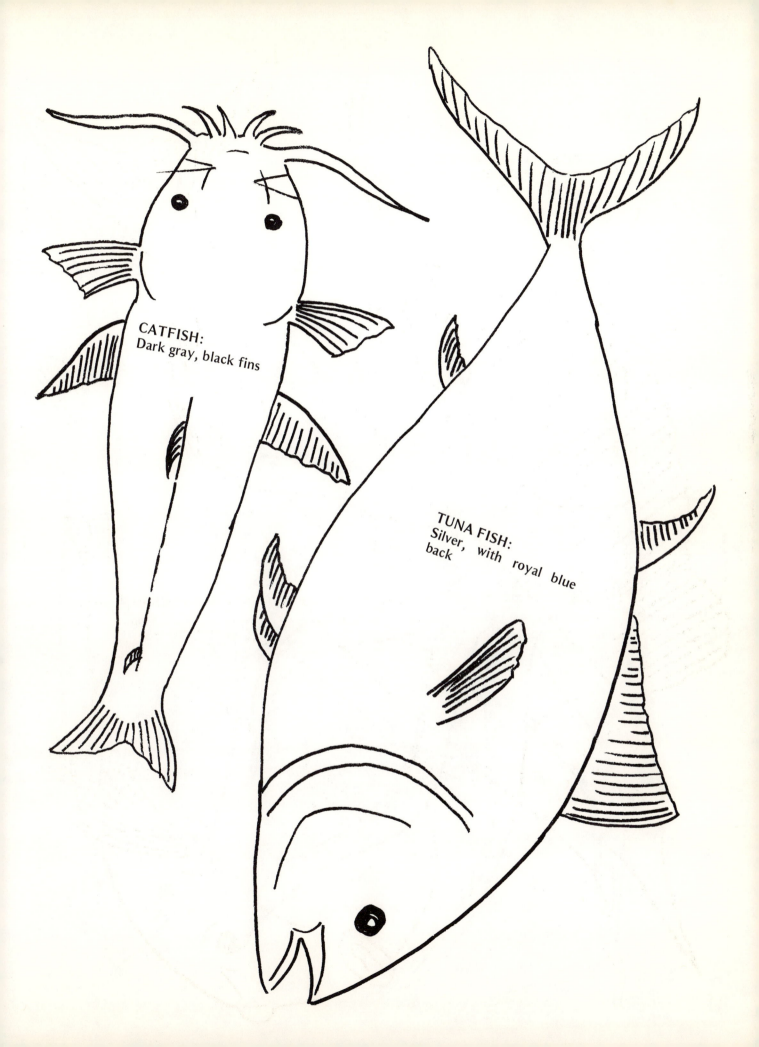

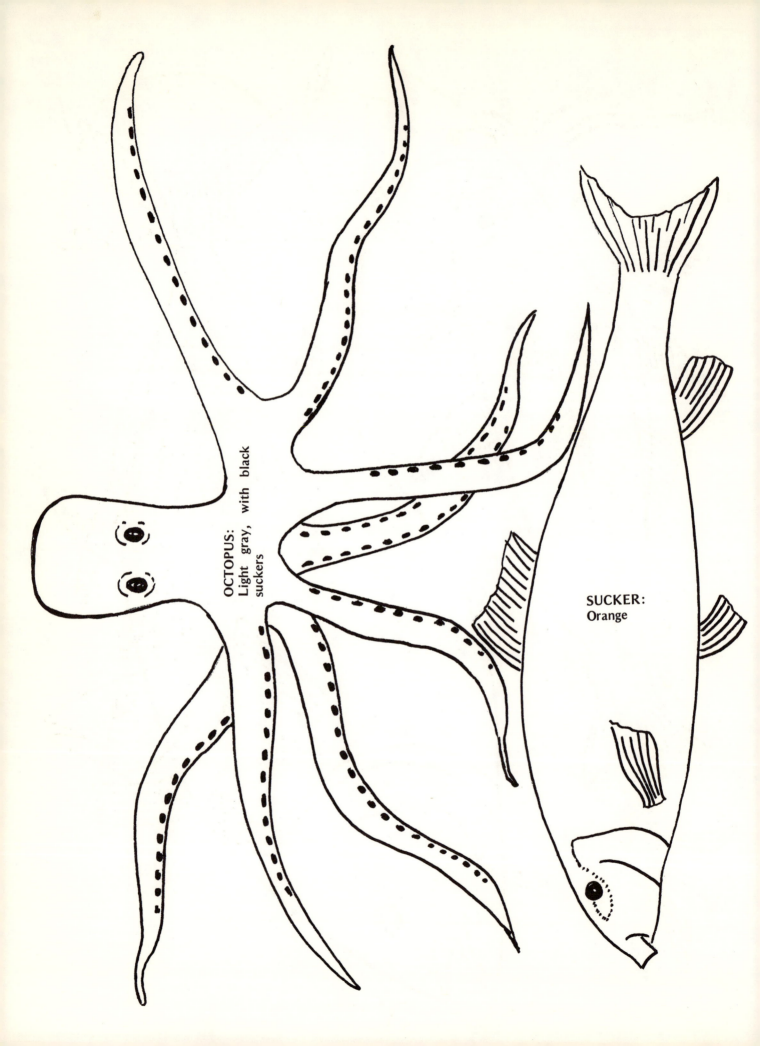

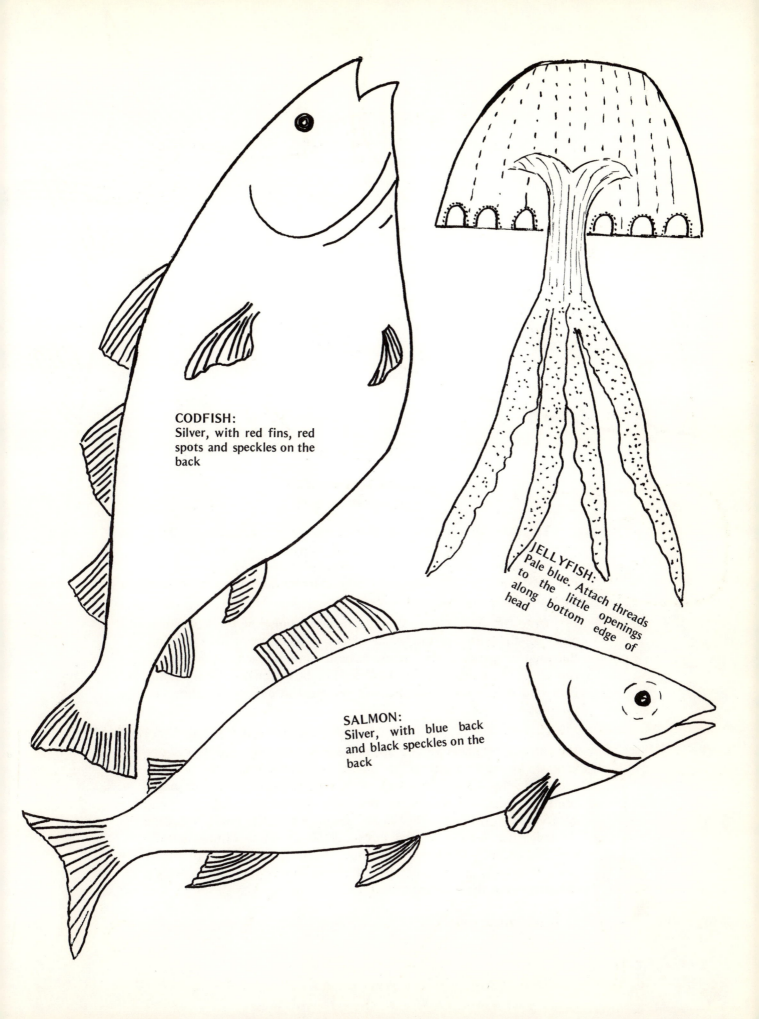

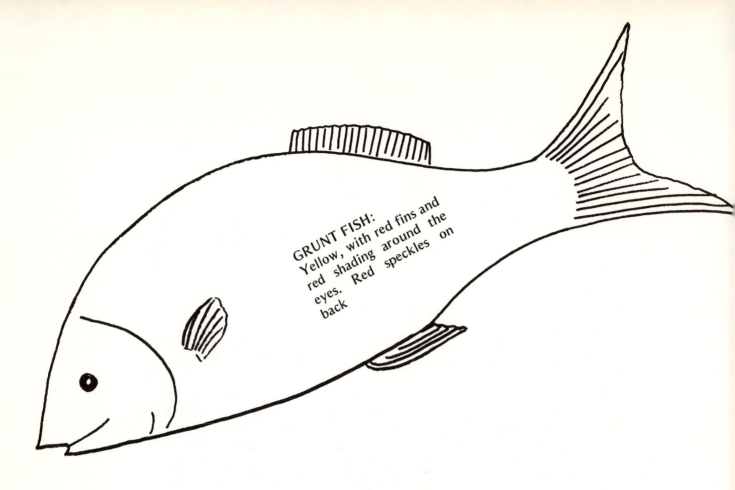

GRUNT FISH:
Yellow, with red fins and red shading around the eyes. Red speckles on back

A STORY TO PREPARE
(using a word-picture)

The flannelgraph story below is called a word-picture story. When you read a story in which the main object or a simple scene is something that can be taken apart and reassembled piece by piece, this is a good story to tell using the word-picture method. Here are instructions for preparing a story of this nature.

Write the story out in simple language. Underline the key words. Make all the parts for the theme object or picture you have in mind. Put the key words on the pieces. As you come to each key word, put the piece on which it is written on the board. When finished, the complete object on the board will remind the children of the main point of the story.

Use this method to tell the story of Ahab and Jezebel below. From the patterns on pages 52 and 53, make your grapevine and twenty-one grapes. On the first leaf, print "Ahab"; on the second, "Jezebel"; on the third, "King & Queen"; and on the bough, "Israel." On each grape, print an underlined word from the story. Number the grapes. As you come to each italicized word in the story, put on the board the grape on which that word is written. Put six grapes on the first line under the vine and decrease the number of grapes by one in each of the following rows. When you are finished you will have a cluster of grapes to remind the children of the vineyard of Naboth.

50 ■ SOMETHING TO SEE

Naboth's Vineyard
I Kings 21:1-20

Jezebel and Ahab were king and queen of Israel. They had more than they needed, but they were never *satisfied*. (1) One day Ahab looked out onto a beautiful *vineyard* (2) near his palace. He *wanted* (3) it very much. So, he went over to *Naboth* (4) and said, "*Give me* (5) your vineyard so I can grow my herbs in it. I will give you a better vineyard or the *money* (6) for it." But Naboth did *not* want to *sell* (7) his vineyard. It had been handed down to him from his forefathers and he wanted to keep it for his *children*. (8) Ahab went home very *cross*. (9) He lay down on his bed and *sulked* (10) because he couldn't have Naboth's vineyard.

Soon *Jezebel* (11) came home. "Why are you sad, Ahab?" she asked. "I *want* (12) Naboth's vineyard and he won't let me have it," Ahab answered. "Don't worry, I *will get* (13) it for you," said the queen.

So Jezebel sat down and wrote a *letter* (14), requesting that Naboth be *killed*. (15) As soon as Naboth was dead, Jezebel came to Ahab and said, "The vineyard is yours, Naboth is *dead*." (16) So Ahab and Jezebel *took* (17) Naboth's vineyard for their own.

But *God* (18) was very *angry*. (19) He sent the prophet *Elijah* (20) to tell them they were going to die terrible deaths because of their great *wickedness*. (21)

Telling a story this way can be fun as well as educational. You will find it best for children who can read. More stories you might construct with this method are "The Tower of Babel," Genesis 11:1-9 (build a tower stone by stone or layer by layer); "Joseph's Coat," Genesis 37:1-4 (construct a coat with colored strips or patches); "The Good Shepherd," John 10:1-18 (make a sheepfold in sections and enough sheep for the remainder of the key words); "The Woman at the Well," John 4:1-41 (write the key words on stones to build a well; set a bucket by the completed well); and "The Parable of the Talents," Matthew 25:14-30 (make a sack which is tipping over; have gold coins spilling out). Can you think of other stories you could tell with word pictures?

GRAPEVINE PATTERN FOR "NABOTH'S VINEYARD"

SUGGESTIONS FOR FILING PRINTED FLANNELGRAPH STORIES

Because there are usually several stories to tell with the figures in each packet you buy, you can't file this type of story separately. Instead, you might do the following:

1. Prepare two folders, one for manufactured flannelgraph stories—O.T. and one for manufactured flannelgraph stories—N.T. (See p. 128.)

2. File packets in their Biblical order within the folders.

3. Be sure to put stars on the cards made out for each story you can tell with your packages.

4. Put overlays and background scenes in plastic bags. Label each bag. Store them in a labeled box.

SUGGESTIONS FOR FILING HOMEMADE FLANNELGRAPH STORIES

1. Put all the parts of the story into an envelope.

2. Put the written story and the envelope of pieces into a file folder, labeled and filed like the stories in chapter 4.

6

PUPPETS

Having a set of puppets dressed like Biblical characters will help you teach stories in which there is much body movement and conversation among the characters. To be ready to tell any number of stories with your set, it should include:

A young man	A girl
A young woman	A boy
An old man	A king
An old woman	A queen
An angel	A few extra men

MATERIALS YOU WILL NEED

Puppet patterns on pages 61–65
About 1½ yards (36" wide) of heavy white or beige material
About ¾ yard (36" wide) of white or beige felt
Sewing scraps

HOW TO MAKE A SET OF PEOPLE

First, make complete paper patterns for the basic body and clothing patterns. (You will notice that only one side of each pattern appears on the pattern sheets.) Cut the basic body pattern through two thicknesses of material. Unbleached calico is very good. Cut the hands and face from felt. At the ends of the arms, lay the hands between the material, facing the center of the pattern with the thumbs pointing upward. Sew around the pattern with a 3/8" seam. Clip the curves and turn the puppet inside out.

Make a face on the felt circle. Use buttons, colored felt, embroidery thread, or magic markers. Tack the face onto the puppet. Make hair and beard (if required) from wool (yarn), cotton wool (cotton batting), light steel wool, doll or real hair, felt, and such things. Tack them onto the head where required. If the puppet is wearing a head cover, you needn't put hair on the back of the head.

To dress the puppet, cut a garment from your clothing pattern through two thicknesses of heavy material. Stripes, weaves, and plain materials are good. Notice some of the clothing styles you might try on page 64, or in Bible pictures you may have. If you cut material with pinking shears, it will not fray. If you have none, hem all the raw edges. Sew the costume in the style you desire and decorate it to fit the character wearing it. Tack the garment in place on the body to prevent it from slipping around when telling a story. Use your imagination and make each puppet unique. The children will love them!

You might make a few extra garments to keep your characters varied as you use your puppets for different stories.

To manipulate these puppets, it is good to put the index and middle fingers into the head, the ring and baby fingers into one arm, and the thumb into the other arm.

HOW TO MAKE ANIMALS

Sometimes animal characters are needed in puppet stories. They don't usually speak; but in the puppet story in this chapter, the donkey does speak! Instructions are given below for making a donkey puppet. You can make many other animals in the same way.

Notice the donkey in the photograph on pages 58 and 59 and in diagram 3-B on page 61. To make the head, take a rectangular sheet of gray or brown paper 12" x 18". Fold the paper in three sections lengthwise. Fold the long strip into a "W" formation. See diagram 3-A on page 61. Using the patterns on the same page, cut the ears, eyes, and tongue from colored paper. Fold the eyes on the dotted lines. Paste them onto the top of the head so that they stand away slightly. Overlap the two bottom corners of each ear and staple them closed. Draw the nose lines and nostrils. Paste the flat edge of the tongue inside the mouth, near the fold.

To make a neck, cut a rectangular piece of material 11" x 14". Fold the material in half lengthwise. Make a mane from paper, using two strips 2" x 10". Along one edge, cut slits close together, ¾ of the way across the strips. Lay the mane between the material, the uncut edge even with the two edges of the folded material. Sew the material and paper together with a ½" seam. Turn the neck inside out. With the mane going down the center, staple the top edge of the neck to the top corners of the head. Staple the ears in place.

To manipulate the puppet, put your arm into the neck, your fingers inside the fold of the top of the head, and your thumb in the fold of the bottom of the head. Work the mouth open and closed.

In addition to using animal puppets in Bible stories, they can also be used for preschool and primary children to tell application stories (see chap. 10), to converse with the children, sing songs, make announcements, and so forth.

TIPS FOR TELLING PUPPET STORIES

1. Know your story well. Tell it; don't read it.
2. Have all the puppet characters placed in the order you will be using them in the story.
3. Practice the story in front of a mirror.

A STORY TO PREPARE

To tell this story, you could use many puppets. But since you are just beginning to use puppets, let's use only two. Notice them in the photograph. Make Balaam an older man with a beard. Make the donkey from the instructions given. Read the whole story until you know it well. Practice telling it in simple words. Then practice telling it with your puppets. Let the table top be your stage. Manipulate the puppets as suggested. Add any other gestures you like.

If you prefer to go into more detail, use other puppets to represent the King of Moab, the two sets of messengers he sends to Balaam, and the angel. Use puppet stands like those described on page 60 to hold the extra characters in the scene. If you use just the two puppets, however, tell the story up to verse 21 before you begin to use the puppets in the incidents given in the following outline.

King Balak Sends for Balaam

Numbers 22:1-35

1. Balaam gets up and saddles his donkey. Put the donkey on the right hand, Balaam on the left. Bend Balaam forward to pick up an imaginary saddle from the table and straighten him up as he puts the saddle on the donkey. To make him climb on the donkey, cross your left wrist over your right one.

2. As the donkey walks along, move your right arm up and down.

3. When the donkey meets the angel the first two times, swerve your arm toward the children.

4. Make Balaam beat the donkey with his hand when appropriate.

5. When the invisible angel appears the third time, have the donkey collapse on the table.

6. When the donkey speaks to Balaam, turn his head back to Balaam and work his mouth open and closed.

7. When Balaam sees the angel, take him off the donkey and have him lie face down on the table, before getting up to speak his closing words of the story.

8. Put him back on his donkey as he goes on to the king.

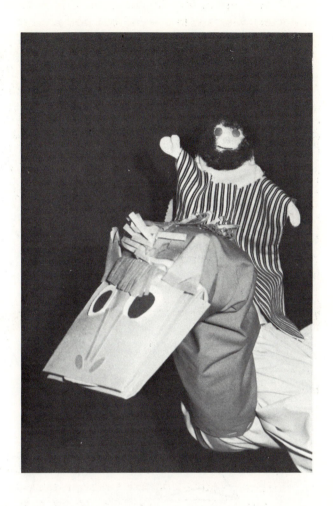

There are so many Bible stories you could tell with puppets. Here are a few: "Stories from the Book of Ruth;" "The Early Life of Samuel," I Samuel 1–3; "A Slave Girl Helps Naaman," II Kings 5:1-14; "The Temptations of Jesus," Matthew 4:1011; Mark 1:12-13; Luke 4:1-14; "The Cripple at the Pool of Bethesda," John 5:1-18; "The Good Samaritan," Luke 10:25-37; and "An Angel Lets Peter Out of Prison," Acts 12:1-23.

If you had nothing more than a table top, a few props, and a set of puppets, you could tell many, many stories with wonderful effect. But if you are interested in making an elaborate stage and props, you can find instructions in *Bible Storytelling Puppets,* by Evelyn Mitchell.

A very useful idea in this book is how to make stands for extra characters who are in a scene but not active on your hands. Notice diagram 2. To make a stand, grasp the hook of a wire coat hanger in one hand and the center of the bottom in the other. Pull till the two side corners are about 6" apart. Then bend the bottom "V" back at the corners. Close the hook into a circle. As you can see from the diagram, this makes an excellent stand.

DIAGRAM 2

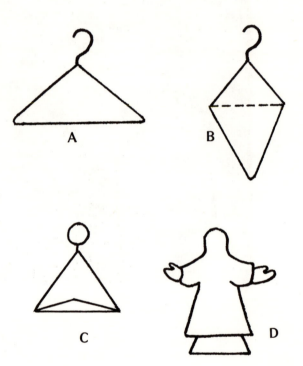

SUGGESTIONS FOR FILING

1. Put each puppet into a plastic bag.
2. Put extra garments into a separate bag.
3. Keep puppet set in a labeled box.
4. Write "Puppets" under "Methods" on the cards of those stories which you could tell effectively with puppets.
5. Put red stars on these cards if your puppet set is ready to use.

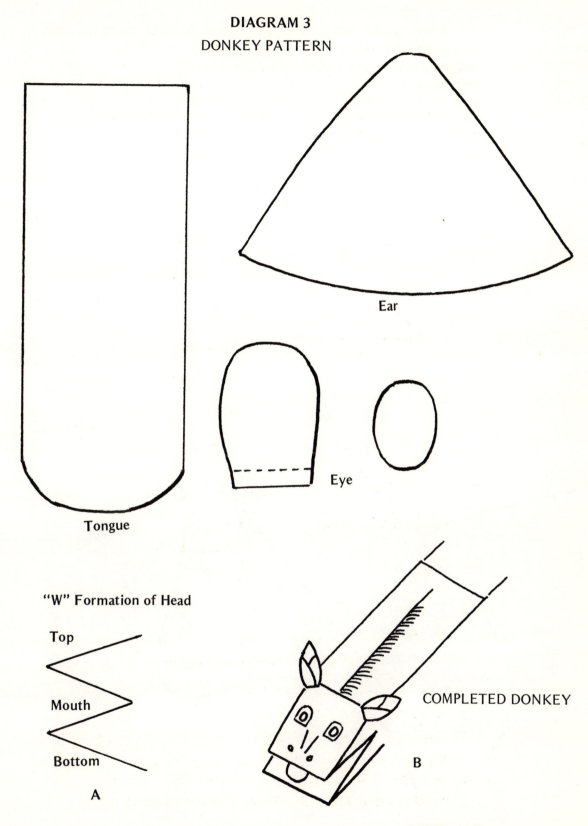

DIAGRAM 3
DONKEY PATTERN

Ear

Eye

Tongue

"W" Formation of Head

Top
Mouth
Bottom

A

COMPLETED DONKEY

B

PUPPETS ▪ 61

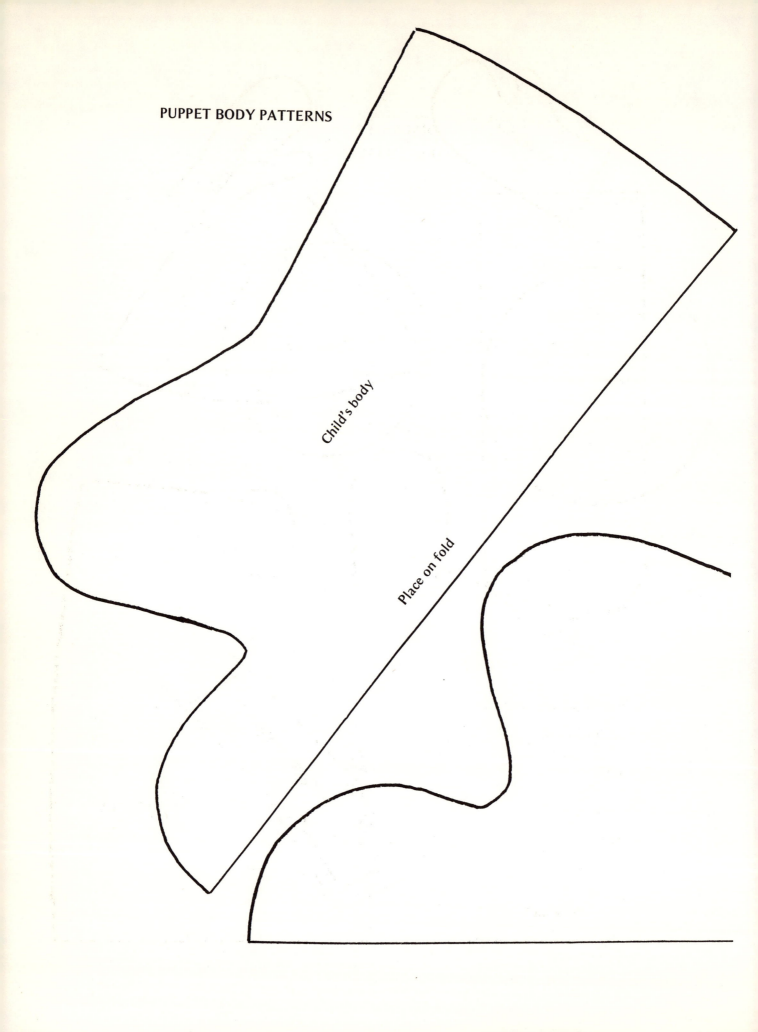

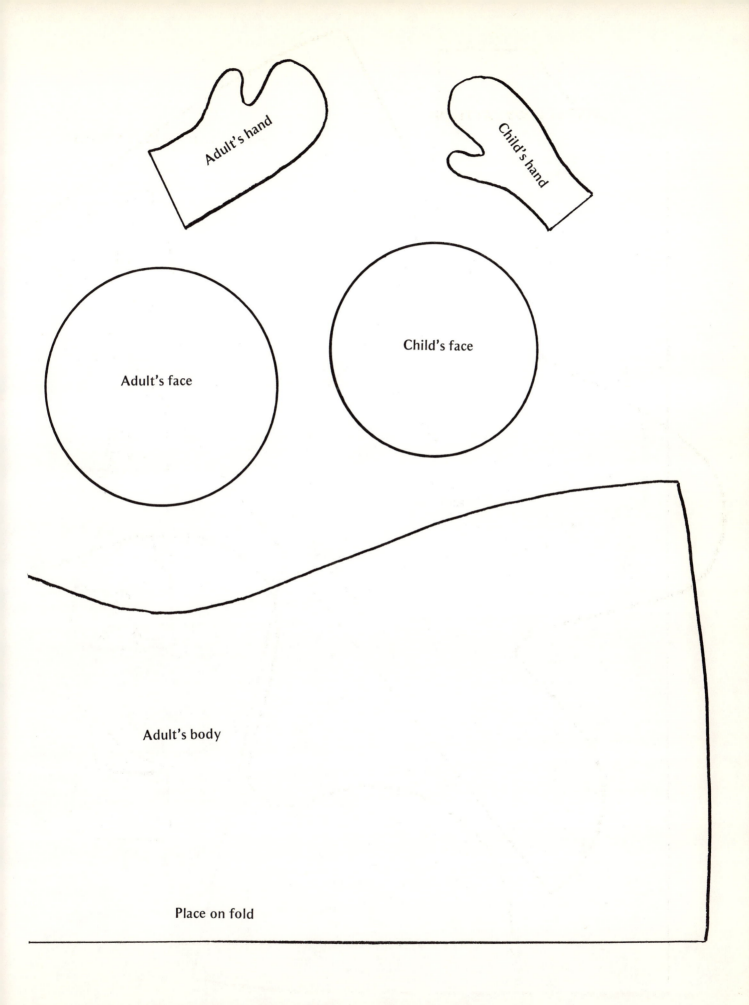

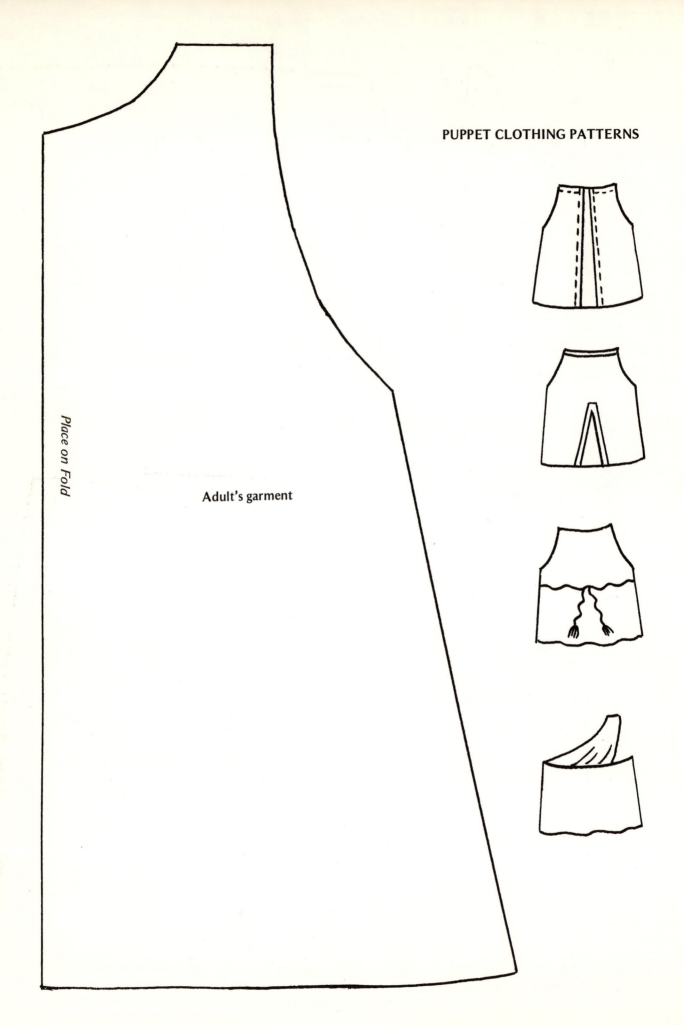

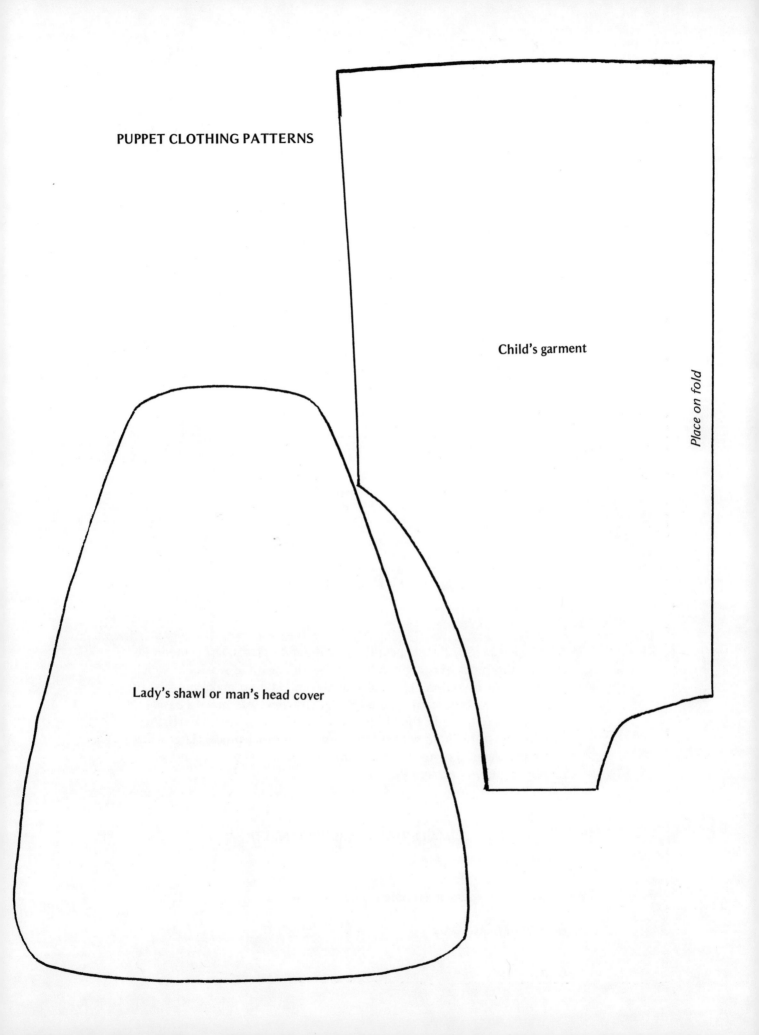

7

MODELS

Models are small-scale people, animals, and objects. Using models is perhaps the most exciting way to tell historical Bible stories in which there is a lot of action. There are numerous ways to make models. In this chapter we will learn a simple, inexpensive way to make a basic set of models like those in the photograph. These can be used interchangeably in any stories told with this method. Add other models later when you need them. Try to use the same style and keep your models in proportion as you expand the set.

MATERIALS YOU WILL NEED

Model Patterns on pages 77–84
12 large cardboard cylinders from bathroom tissue
Colored paper (pregummed paper is good)

*6 slightly smaller bathroom tissue cylinders
A few sheets of stiff cardboard (not corrugated)
White pipe cleaners

*The length of a large or small cylinder is about 4½". The difference lies in the diameter of the two rolls.

HOW TO MAKE PEOPLE

A basic set of people might include the same characters as those in your puppet set.

Refer to pages 76 and 77. To make a person, trace the basic body pattern onto stiff cardboard. Cut it out. Cut the face and hands from pink or beige paper. (For face patterns, turn to p. 78.) Paste them onto the body. Cut hair or shawl from the patterns and paste them into place. Leave the bottom edges of the shawl, beard, and little girl's hair loose. This will allow you to stick the clothing on right up to the neck.

Using colored paper or cloth, trace and cut out clothing. Just retrace the basic body pattern up to the bottom of the neck. Decorate the garment at the neck and around the sleeve edges if you like. Paste the clothing onto both sides of the body.

For the base of the body, prepare a cylinder the required size given on the basic body pattern sheet (p. 77). Cut a rectangular piece of

DIAGRAM 4

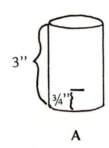

A

B

C

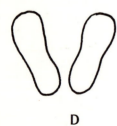

D

colored paper or cloth the length of the cylinder by about 7". Staple or glue it around the cylinder. Slip the completed body into the covered cylinder. The model is ready to use.

Try to vary the face features, hair coloring, and clothing on the characters.

You will want to use your model characters interchangeably in different stories. The following are some suggestions for doing so. Change outside garments by using different cylinders. Make some beards and headgear removable. To attach them when needed, you could use plastic adhesive or small pieces of masking tape rolled into circles, sticky side out. Add crowns and wings whenever they are needed. If you make a character with white inner and outer garments you can use him as an angel with wings or as another character with a different outer garment.

To make a figure sitting down, prepare a cylinder about 3" in length with a slit cut ¾" from one end. See diagram 4-A. Trace completely around the outside edge of the pattern given for a pair of camel's legs on page 83. Note diagram 4-B. Cover the cylinder and legs pattern to match. Bend the legs about the middle to form knees. Insert the legs into the slit you have cut (diagram 4-C). Paste two feet soles to the bottom edge of the garment (diagrams 4-C and D). If you want to have the same character stand and sit in a story, you can make a whole cylinder to match the one you have prepared for the character when he is sitting down. Then you will simply need to switch the body from one cylinder to another to change positions.

DIAGRAM 5

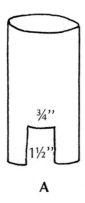

A

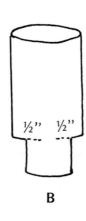

B

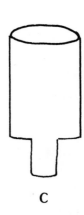

C

D

E

To make a soldier, cut away a piece of full length cylinder on both sides as shown in diagram 5-A. Extend the horizontal cut ½" both directions on the remaining two side pieces of the cylinder (diagram 5-B). Carefully bend the two sides of each piece until they come together evenly (diagram 5-C). Staple them closed, making two legs (diagram 5-D). Glue feet to the bottom of the legs, centering each foot. Use the feet patterns given on page 81. If the body doesn't stand firmly, check to see if the bottom edges of the legs are level, adjust the position of the feet, or make them a little larger. (You could use these same instructions to make the body cylinder for any figure who is wearing a short garment.)

Cover the cylinder in two sections to make the soldier's costume. (See diagram 5-E.) Paste strips of silver paper or tin foil on the top half to make the armor. Cover the bottom half with a skirt of paper or slightly gathered material.

Prepare the body using the patterns on page 81. Make the shoulder straps silver like the rest of the coat of armor. Likewise, cut the helmet from silver paper, using whichever pattern you prefer. Attach a spear to the soldier's hand whenever it is required. It would be best to leave soldiers clean shaven.

HOW TO MAKE ANIMALS

A basic set of animals common in Bible days might include:

DIAGRAM 6

A donkey   A goat
A camel   An ox
A sheep   *A pig
A lamb

*Jews didn't have pigs around the house, but there are many references to them in Scripture.

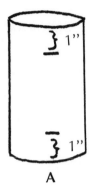

A

Once you have made one of each type of animal, you can easily make duplicates for stories in which you need more than one of any kind.

To make an animal's body, cut a cylinder to the required length given on the animal head pattern sheet (p. 82). Cover it with colored paper just as you were instructed to cover the base of the body for a person. For sheep and lambs, stick white cotton batting (also called cotton wool) on the body cylinder.

Trace and cut out the head pattern three times, once on stiff cardboard, twice on colored paper. To trace the features on the colored paper for both sides of the animal's head, first trace the pattern in this book onto the back of the pattern sheet. Now trace the features for the left side of the head from the back side of the pattern, and features for the right side of the head from the front side of the pattern. (You will see what I mean when you try it.) Paste the head pieces together. Cut the slit through all three thicknesses, being careful not to cut it too wide.

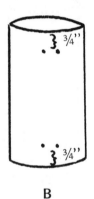

B

Trace and cut out the leg pattern six times, twice on stiff cardboard, four times on colored paper. Notice the different lengths for each animal's legs. Paste the colored legs on both sides of each set of cardboard legs.

Look at diagram 6-A on this page. To attach the legs to the body, cut two slits, ¼" wide, in the ends of the body cylinder. Use a sharp knife. Cut them directly opposite one another, one inch from each end of the cylinder.

To make legs for sheep and goats, use pipe cleaners. Cut a pipe cleaner 4½" long for each pair of sheep legs; 4" long for lambs; and 4½" long for goats. Using an old ball point pen, pierce two holes for each pair of legs in the end of the body cylinder. (See diagram 6-B.) For the lamb, make the holes ½" from each end of the cylinder. Thread

70 ■ SOMETHING TO SEE

the pipe cleaner through the two holes. Twist the two sides together right up under the body cylinder, making both legs equal length. Make a second pair of legs the same way. Spread each pair of legs out under the knot so the animal will stand.

Leave pipe cleaner legs white for sheep and lambs. Wrap them with colored wool (yarn) for goats. To wrap a pair of legs, start at the knot under the body. Wrap the wool around the knot and down one leg until it is completely covered. Break the wool. Run a darning needle a few stitches up the leg. Thread the wool into the needle eye. Pull the wool and needle through the wrapped wool and cut the remaining end of the wool off neatly. Stitching into the leg this way will prevent the wool from unraveling.

Tails can be made in a variety of ways. For a camel or an ox, make a tail from the pattern. You might make the tail tassel and the camel's hump tops a different color from the rest of the animal. For example, make the camel light brown and his hump tops and tail tassel dark brown. Paste the tail just inside the top of the cylinder and let it hang down. For the other animals, pierce a hole at the top edge of the body cylinder. Then—for goats and donkeys—thread a few pieces of colored wool through the hole and tie them in a knot. For sheep or lambs, use short pieces of pipe cleaner for tails. To make a pig's tail, use a piece of curly wire.

Cut the two camel's humps and hump tops from colored paper. Cut slits along the dotted lines. Make the humps into cones and staple them shut. Paste the tops onto the humps. Staple the humps to the camel's back so they overlap. Let the first one overlap the edge of the body enough to cover over the piece jutting up behind the camel's head when it is in place.

Assemble the complete animal and stand it up.

HOW TO MAKE SCENERY

Notice the scenery patterns on page 84. Although they are only half patterns, they are ready to use as they are. To make an object, fold two sheets of colored paper in half. On the fold trace a pattern for the desired object. Cut it out through all four thicknesses of paper. Open out the complete object. There will be two copies. Staple the two pieces together down the center fold. Bend the four sides so they all go different directions. These objects will stand and are very authentic looking.

Make up several bushes, a tree, and a fire. You can make patterns for other objects as you need them. When you make the tree, staple or glue the two tops to the two bottoms. Then lay them back together again and staple the completed trees down the center fold.

HOW TO MAKE HOUSES AND OTHER CONSTRUCTIONS

Fit boxes of many varieties into the shape of the building or construction you wish to make. Tape the boxes into place with masking tape. Cover the whole construction with strips of newspaper smeared with wheat paste or flour-water glue. Allow this to dry and paint it with enamel or tempera paint. Or paper it with appropriate wallpaper. Shade in doors, windows, and so forth, or cut them from colored paper and paste them on.

Look at the house in the photograph on page 67. Make a house from Bible days, using the box construction techniques we have just described. Make it in proportion to the size of your model characters. A house in Bible days was usually made of brick. The roof was flat and there was often a wall around it. To make the staircase and the wall around the roof, use strips of stiff cardboard, bent to the required shape. Tape them onto the structure with masking tape. A Bible house often had a small guest room on the roof. In some stories there is action on the roof, so it is a good idea to make the guest room removable. Make it up separately to rest on the roof when you need it. A side room might be added to the house, too, as you see in the photograph.

On page 84 you will find patterns for windows and doors. Cut little pieces of paper to make brick trimming over the doorways.

You can invent many other constructions as you need them. The patterns presented in this chapter will be sufficient for telling the story below and many others.

TIPS FOR TELLING MODEL STORIES

1. Arrange the basic scene on the tabletop ahead of time.
2. Have a box beside you or under the table. Take characters from it as you need them in the story, and put characters and objects into it when you are finished with them.
3. Tell your story; don't read it.
4. Stand or sit behind or to the side of the scene so you can move the models without blocking the children's view.

A STORY TO PREPARE

For the story below, carefully read Acts 10. Practice telling the story in your own words. Then tell it with models, using the suggestions as you see fit.

The First Gentile Christians
Acts 10

SCENE I—Cornelius has a vision (vv. 1-8)

Models needed: Cornelius (dressed as a soldier), two messengers, a soldier, an angel

Have Cornelius standing alone as you describe him and his family. Let the angel stand before him at the appropriate time. Bring the servants and the soldier to Cornelius as you tell how he sends for Peter.

SCENE II—Peter has a vision (vv. 9-17a)

Models needed: Peter, a woman, a little girl, a fire, a house (without the guest room on the roof), a few sheep eating leaves from a clump of bushes, a white handkerchief or paper napkin, a few small plastic animals (these should be animals Jews were not allowed to eat—e.g., camel, rabbit, pig)

Open the scene with Peter standing on the roof of Simon's house. Have the woman and little girl standing before the fire near the house, preparing lunch. Behind the house, away from the view of the class, have the napkin full of plastic animals ready. Lift it into the air and set it down in front of Peter on the roof. Let it fall open so the children can see the animals inside. Repeat this vision three times. Then remove the sheet from sight, leaving Peter to ponder the meaning of the dream.

SCENE III—Cornelius's messengers arrive at Simon's house (vv. 17b-23)

Models needed: All the models used in Scene II, except the sheet of animals; the three messengers from Cornelius

Have the messengers of Cornelius approach the scene and stand off to the side as if outside the gate. Bring Peter down from the roof and have him go to the messengers to see what they want. Have them all come and stand in front of the house. If the door to your house can be opened, have the messenger and Peter enter the house to spend the night inside. If not, just tell this incident while the scene remains as it is, with the messengers talking to Peter. The next day, have Peter and the messengers prepare to leave for Caesarea.

SCENE IV—Peter goes to Cornelius (vv. 24-28)

Models needed: Peter, Cornelius, the messengers, a tree, some bushes

Have Cornelius standing by a tree. Let Peter and the messengers approach him. Have Cornelius come to meet them and bow down to the ground before Peter. Stand him up again as Peter speaks to him. Let the scene remain like this as you tell the rest of the story.

You could divide this story after Scene II and use it as the basis for two lessons. This would be wise for younger children, especially.

When telling stories with models it is not necessary to represent every character mentioned in each incident. However, be sure to tell the story as it is. The children will understand that others were present in the scene, even though they are not being featured. For instance, it would not be practical to have the six Jewish Christians (Acts 11:12) from Joppa accompany Peter and the messengers to Caesarea. Likewise, when Peter meets Cornelius in Caesarea, the account says there were relatives and friends waiting there with Cornelius. It would not only be a great deal of work to prepare more characters, but it would also be difficult to handle all of them on the "stage" at one time.

In Scene II, it is suggested you have a woman and a young girl preparing lunch before a fire in front of the house. However, the account says nothing more than the fact that lunch was being prepared. So, you need not have these two characters in the scene unless you like the idea.

If you would prefer to tell only part of the story with models, you could do so. Scene II contains the most action and would be the best single scene to work on. When you are telling a fairly lengthy part of a story without models, it is a good idea to move away from the scene you have prepared so the children will not be distracted while you continue or conclude the story. This is especially important if you are telling the first part of the story without visual aids.

As you prepare a model story, you will want to divide it into scenes if it is a long story. List the models you will need in each scene and jot down the actions you intend to use. You will not likely need to look at this information while you are telling the story to the class, but it will help you organize your thoughts and material ahead of time so your story will go smoothly.

Some other stories you might tell using models are these: "Abraham's Strange Visitors," Genesis 18; "Abraham Offers Isaac," Genesis 22:1-19; "Moses and the Burning Bush," Exodus 3—4; "The Lost Sheep," Matthew 18:12-13; Luke 15:3-7; "The Woman at the Well," John 4:1-42; and "The Transfiguration," Matthew 17:1-13; Mark 9:2-13; Luke 9:28-36.

SUGGESTIONS FOR FILING

1. Disassemble all the removable parts of the characters.
2. Fold all scenery pieces flat.
3. Lay all flat pieces in an envelope.
4. Stand all cylinders on end.
5. Put the complete set into a box and label it.
6. Reassemble the set whenever you need it.
7. Under "Methods," write "Models" on the cards of those Bible stories you could tell effectively with your set. When you have completed your set, put red stars on these cards.

USING VISUALIZED STORIES WITH DIFFERENT AGE GROUPS

If you were presenting Bible stories to a mixed age group of children ranging from two to twelve years of age, you could use any of the methods of story telling we have studied in the last four chapters. However, it is unusual for a teacher to have a class in which there are all age groups present. Therefore, we will mention some suggestions for using these methods with different age groups.

Preschool children will thoroughly enjoy stories told with any of the visual aids we have discussed, except those in word-picture stories. You can use visual aids to tell every story to preschoolers. It will help keep their attention, as well as help them learn more effectively. Keep your language simple when telling stories, and when you use pictures they should not be too detailed.

Primary children will enjoy stories that are taught with all the visual aids we have studied. It is good to use some type of visual aid with each story you tell them, if possible.

Junior children do not need to see visual aids for every story they hear. However, they will enjoy any of the types of visual aids we have studied whenever you use them. Notice the suggestions on page 99 under "Acting out Stories" for using puppets and models with juniors.

You might let junior children make a display of models when studying a theme such as "Preaching the Gospel in All the World" or "The Antediluvian Period." In the first one, let each child make a model of a foreign person, using the same techniques as we learned for making Bible people. In the second, have each child make an animal and let someone make an ark for a display of "Noah and the Ark."

Try to vary the types of visual aids you use. However, if you are teaching a series of stories on the life of a Bible character, you might use the same method for all those stories. For example, you could teach the life of Job using models for each story.

GENERAL TIPS FOR TELLING BIBLE STORIES

1. Adapt your language to the age group you are teaching.
2. Give the meaning of all new or difficult words before the story.
3. On a map, point out the area where the story occurred (for juniors only).
4. Explain the customs mentioned.
5. Read or quote other Scripture verses that help explain the story.
6. Apply the principle of the story to life today (see chap. 10).
7. Retell the story if there is time.

BASIC BODY PATTERNS FOR PEOPLE

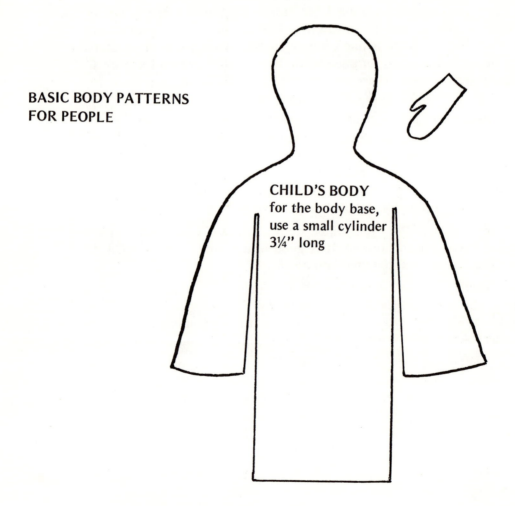

CHILD'S BODY for the body base, use a small cylinder 3¼" long

BASIC BODY PATTERNS FOR PEOPLE

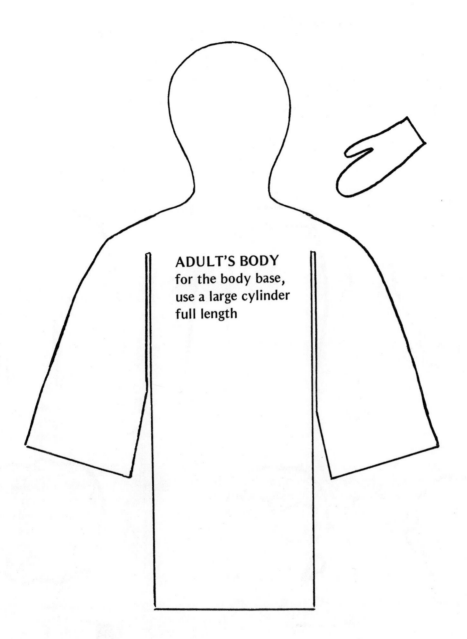

ADULT'S BODY
for the body base, use a large cylinder full length

MODELS ■ 77

HEAD PATTERNS FOR PEOPLE

ADDITIONAL HEAD PATTERNS

80 ■ SOMETHING TO SEE

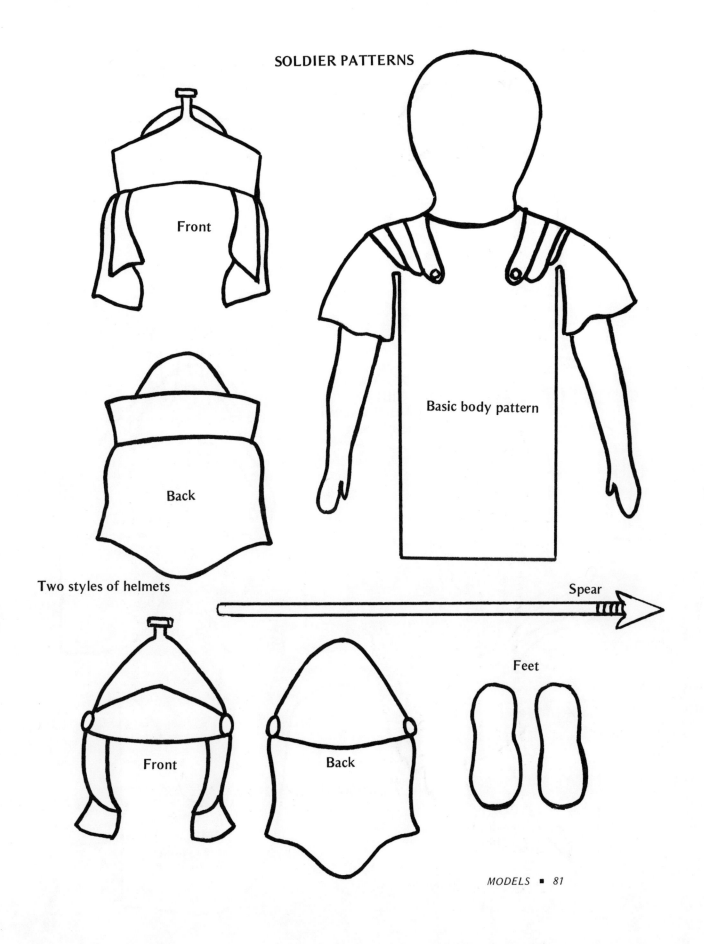

HEAD PATTERNS FOR ANIMALS

BODY PARTS FOR ANIMALS

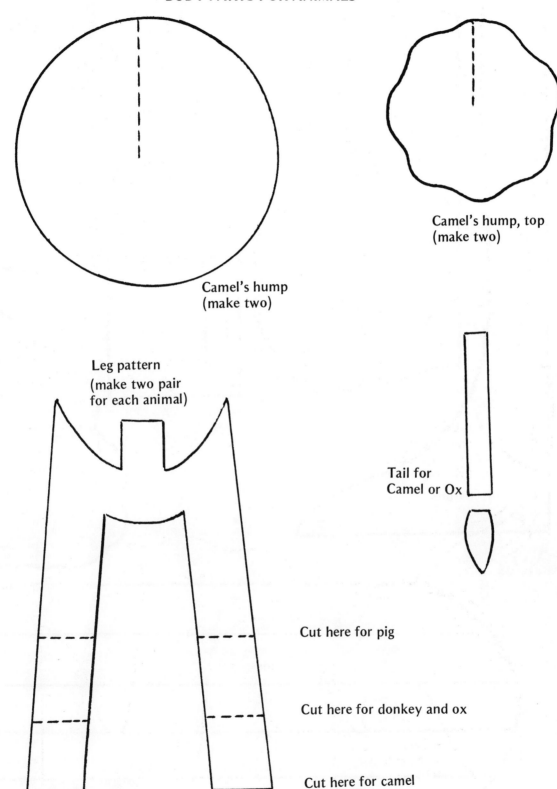

Camel's hump
(make two)

Camel's hump, top
(make two)

Leg pattern
(make two pair
for each animal)

Tail for
Camel or Ox

Cut here for pig

Cut here for donkey and ox

Cut here for camel

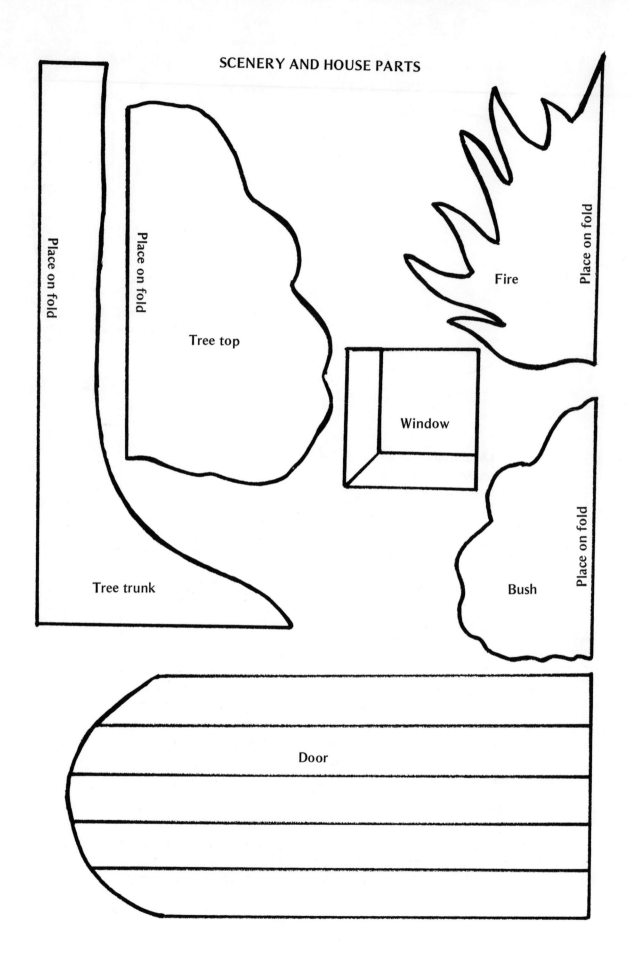

8

DECORATING THE CLASSROOM TO EMPHASIZE A THEME

The theme of a unit is that which all of the stories have in common. As we discussed in chapter 2, this can be either a period of history, a certain subject, or a moral. You can emphasize this theme by making your bulletin board display and attendance charts into pictures that represent it. Below are instructions for making these displays.

HOW TO PREPARE A THEME BULLETIN BOARD DISPLAY

Think of a simple scene that depicts the theme of the unit. Work out a caption or heading for the scene. It might be a phrase, part of a verse of Scripture, or the unit title. Make it short. Draw a sketch of the complete scene. Prepare the objects for the scene from colored paper. Cut letters for the caption from letter patterns traced on colored paper.

Put up the display before the first lesson in the unit. Make the background with crepe paper or other paper that comes on rolls or in long sheets. Use staples, thumb tacks, or straight pins to mount the display. Center the letters of the caption by putting the middle letter in the center of the board first and then working both directions.

Take the display down at the end of the unit.

An example of a theme bulletin board display might be one for a series on the life of Christ, entitled "Following in Christ's Footsteps." Notice the sketch below. The background might be blue sky and sandy beach, made from crepe paper. Cut silhouettes for Jesus, a set of footprints for Him, and a small child from colored paper. Or draw and color in these figures for the display. You could easily find a picture of a little girl to copy from a coloring book, and you might enlarge a flannelgraph figure to represent Jesus. Put Jesus on the left side of the board, the child on the right, and the set of footprints between them.

HOW TO PREPARE THEME ATTENDANCE CHARTS

Make a picture or object which represents the unit. Arrange it so that part of the object lifts up to reveal the attendance record underneath.

Make an attendance record for each child for the whole unit or the part of the unit the chart is to be used for. The sheets must be small enough to be concealed in place on the chart. Paste stickers related to the theme or shiny stars on the sheet(s) each week. Keep the stickers in a box in the classroom. Let the child take his record home at the end of the unit.

In the two photographs below, we have an example of a theme attendance chart. In a unit on mission work for juniors, we studied the activities of missionaries on each continent. In April we were studying the countries under communist control. The only way we can preach to people in many of these lands is by radio. Notice how the object relates to the mission theme. The attendance stickers are small scenes from Bible stories. This also helps emphasize the need to teach the Bible to others. There were twenty-five children in the class, so there were several more sheets behind the one you see in the photograph. At the end of the month, we cut these sheets into strips and the students pasted their strips into the notebooks they had made.

DECORATING THE CLASSROOM TO EMPHASIZE A THEME ■ 87

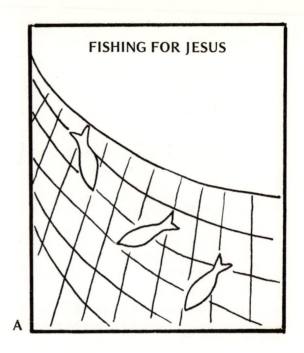

HOW TO INCLUDE ATTENDANCE CHARTS IN YOUR THEME BULLETIN BOARD DISPLAYS

It is often possible to combine this type of attendance chart with the bulletin board display. For example, in the bulletin board display on Christ, you could make each footprint into an individual attendance booklet. Cut one white footprint for each month. Line it and mark in the dates. Staple the three white prints and the colored one together at the top edge. Tack the footprint chart into place on the board. Each child can take his booklet home at the end of the unit.

On pages 91 and 92 there are sketches for four more theme bulletin board displays with attendance charts incorporated into the scenes.

ATTENDANCE BOOSTER CHARTS

Encourage your children to bring visitors. It's fun to keep some kind of a record to which an object can be added for each visitor. It may not be possible to make a chart in keeping with the unit every time, but it is good to do so when you can. In the example we have been using on the life of Christ, you might make a chart like this:

Draw a fish net on a large stiff sheet of cardboard or posterboard. Notice sketch A above. On top of the chart print "Fishing for Jesus." Have a number of small colored fish prepared. Each time a child brings

88 • *SOMETHING TO SEE*

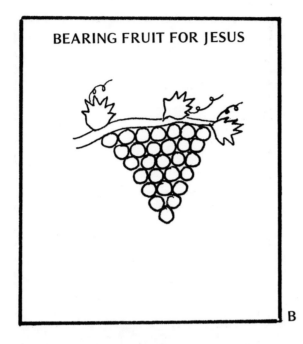

a visitor, print the visitor's name and the name of the child who brought him on a fish. Place the fish in the net on the picture.

Another idea you might use with a theme that stresses evangelism is a fruit tree. Make a large tree with a fluffy green top on a sheet of posterboard. Cut out a supply of one type of fruit. Each time a child brings a visitor put a piece of fruit on the tree.

You might keep a chart like this one up for longer than a unit. You could change the type of fruit from one unit to another.

Using the same caption, you might make a cluster of grapes like the one seen in sketch B. Cut the leaves and bough from colored paper. Using a small glass or lid as a pattern, draw circles under the bough to form a full cluster. On colored paper draw the number of grapes you will need to fill in the empty spaces on the chart. Challenge the children to fill these spaces by bringing visitors.

Here is another suggestion for an attendance booster chart you might make. Entitle it "Leading Others to Jesus." In the center of the poster paste or draw a shepherd to represent Jesus. Cut sheep from white paper and place one sheep in the picture for each visitor a child brings. It would be best to make this picture on a colored background so the sheep would stand out.

From these few suggestions and examples, you can see the beginning of many good teaching possibilities. Let your classroom decorations help you teach!

BULLETIN BOARD—ATTENDANCE CHART

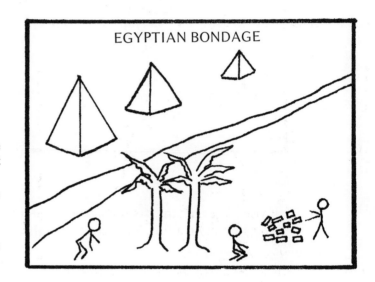

Make the land on the left side of the river sandy-colored; the land on the right side green.

Make a paper chain to represent bondage and string it across the entire scene.

Make people who look like slaves.

Conceal the class attendance chart sheets under the largest pyramid.

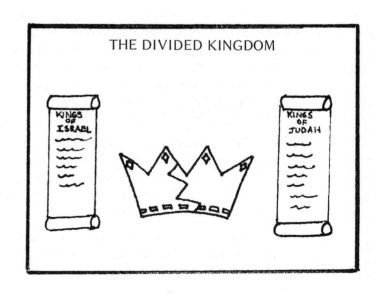

Make the crown of gold paper with costume jewels or jewels made from shiny colored paper.

Make two paper scrolls and mount them on the board. List all the kings so the children will become familiar with them. Then refer to each king in the unit when you come to him.

Have the crown conceal the class attendance sheets.

SKETCHES AND SUGGESTIONS

Make enlarged figures of all the Bible children in the unit. Portray each Bible child holding a placard on which his name is printed.

Conceal the class attendance chart sheets behind the Bible.

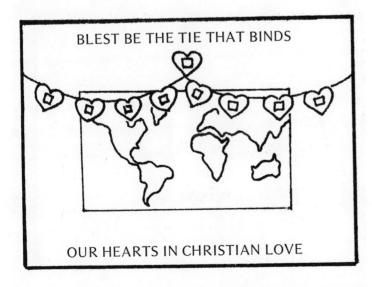

Use this display when teaching a unit on world missions.

Mount a large flat map of the world in the middle of the board.

Make the hearts into individual attendance charts.

Put faces of children of the world on the outside of the hearts.

Put the hearts on a long string and arrange them as shown.

PART THREE

SOMETHING TO DO

9

STORY-CENTERED CLASS ACTIVITIES

As we stated in the introduction, children learn by doing. But *what* are they to learn by doing? They are to learn the Bible stories we teach them and how to use the principles in these stories to build good lives. Just letting children "do" things will not result in very much real learning. The things they do must be related to the Bible story we are teaching during that period. Class activities shouldn't be used as time fillers. They should be centered around the story. In this chapter we will discuss class activities and how they can help the children learn Bible stories and their meanings more effectively.

SINGING

Children in all age groups love to sing. The more children's songs you know, the better you will be able to use songs as a means of helping children learn.

In many songs, the children simply *sing the story*. "Only a Boy Named David," "Daniel Was a Man of Prayer," "Away in a Manger," and "The Wise Man" are a few examples of songs that repeat a story.

Some children's songs *inspire children to imitate* people in a Bible story, or to carry out a Bible principle in their lives. "Dare to Be a Daniel," "This Little Light of Mine," "Roll the Gospel Chariot Along," "I'll Be a Sunbeam," and "I Washed My Hands This Morning" are but a few examples of this type of song.

Many hymns *express the sentiments of Bible stories* we teach the children. Look through your hymnbook sometime and write down a list of songs you think would be suitable for children. Juniors can sing a verse or two of familiar hymns. Preschool and primary children can sing the chorus or a few meaningful lines. A few examples of hymns you could use are "Send the Light," "Joy to the World," "The Lord's My Shepherd," and "Trust and Obey."

Sometimes teachers *make up songs* to go with certain stories. If you would like to try some, use familiar tunes so the children can learn them quickly. Be sure your facts are correct. Here is a song someone made up to use when telling the story of "Noah and the Ark." It is sung to the tune of "Old MacDonald Had a Farm."

"Good Old Noah Built an Ark"

Good old Noah built an ark,
Like God told him to.
And in the ark he placed some cows,
Like God told him to.
With a moo moo here and a moo moo there,
Here a moo, there a moo, everywhere a moo moo.
Good old Noah built an ark,
Like God told him to.

Sing as many verses as you like, giving the children turns to choose the animals. This song is suitable for preschool or primary children.

When you sing new songs in class, introduce them before you sing them, telling how they relate to the Bible story you have just told. Be sure to explain any words or phrases the children might not understand. If a song has actions that go along with it, use them with preschool and primary children.

To teach a new song, or to help make the meaning clear, you might illustrate a song with pictures. For example, little children don't really understand the phrase "Red and yellow, black and white, they are precious in His sight," in the song "Jesus Loves the Little Children." To help them understand, you might show pictures of children of these races as you sing the song. You could use loose pictures to illustrate a song, or make up a large flip chart songbook. You might write the words out for primary and junior children when teaching them a new song.

Do try to choose songs for each lesson that relate to the story in some way. If you have time for a sing-song of miscellaneous songs, sing them before or after the lesson is presented, rather than scattering these unrelated songs throughout the lesson.

ANSWERING QUESTIONS

It is always a good idea to have a question and answer period after each story. This helps the children review and lets you know if you have been understood.

For preschool children, you can simply ask questions and let them answer in turn. However, primary and junior children enjoy different styles of questioning. Here are examples of the most commonly used methods of questioning in their schoolroom:

1. **Fill in the Blank**

    King Ahab wanted a vineyard that belonged to ―――――.

2. **Choose the Correct Word**

    God told Noah to make the ark from (pine, cedar, gopher) wood.

3. **True or False**

    ――Peter was on a rooftop waiting for lunch when God spoke to him in a vision.

4. **Matching**

    This type of questioning is good when you are reviewing the stories in a unit. In a quiz like the example below, have the children match the characters on the left with the incidents on the right. As you can see, all the stories in this quiz are centered around the theme of obedience.

Noah	brought back animals and a king although God had told him to destroy everything.
Abraham	built an ark even though everyone laughed.
Lot's wife	ran away in a ship when God told him to go to Nineveh and preach.
King Saul	was willing to sacrifice his son because God told him to do so.
Daniel	turned into a pillar of salt because she disobeyed God.
Balaam	ate fruit from the tree God told her not to touch.
Jonah	was thrown into a den of lions because he obeyed God.
Eve	was ready to go and curse God's people when God had told him not to go.

If you are not using quarterlies, write down your questions for a lesson in advance. Try not to use the same method every week. Let the children answer the questions orally. Just tell them before you begin which type of questions they are going to have to answer. When using a matching quiz, you will need to print the two columns on the chalkboard so the children can see what is to be matched.

Juniors in particular enjoy being questioned in teams. At the end of a unit you might divide the class into two teams and question the teams in turn, giving two points for each correct answer. If a team misses its question, give the other team a chance to answer for one point. If that team misses, tell the answer yourself and neither team gets a point that round. If you plan to give several team quizzes throughout the year, you might name the teams and keep a little scorecard up in the classroom.

MEMORIZING KEY VERSES

Memorization is still a good way of learning. After you have told and discussed a story, read the most important verse aloud and ask the children to memorize it for the following week. You will need to write the reference down on a slip of paper for smaller children. As the children go through life, verses they have memorized will come back to them over and over again when they are in situations to which these verses apply.

Small children are capable of learning only a few words. Sometimes you will need to reword the phrases so they will be meaningful to them. Older children can learn longer verses, using the exact Biblical wording.

Sometimes it is good to memorize a verse with the children in class. A good way to do this is to break the verse into several parts. Then say aloud, in unison, one phrase at a time. Say the first phrase five times, then the next phrase five times. Then say the two phrases together five times. Carry on like this until you have the whole verse memorized. This is a quick way to memorize and it works well.

Another enjoyable way of memorizing in class is to use picture flash cards. Here is a sample memory verse:

"Thy word is a *lamp* unto my *feet*, and a *light* unto my *path*" (Ps. 119:105).

For each of the italicized words, mount a picture of the object on a stiff sheet of paper. On the back of the sheet, print the part of the verse each picture represents. Read the verse aloud a few times, showing the pictures to the children. Then have the class say each phrase as you show the pictures.

It is not always necessary to have the children memorize a different verse each week. You might use a verse that emphasizes the general theme of the unit several weeks in succession. It is better if the children learn a few important verses well, than it is to memorize many haphazardly.

ACTING OUT STORIES

As we suggested earlier in the course, it is a good idea to retell each Bible story if there is time. Here is another good opportunity for the children to participate. As you retell some stories, small children could move or make noises like the characters. For example, let them be the different animals in "Noah and the Ark." Or, assign them each a role in a story like "The Birth of Jesus." Let them act out their parts as you speak.

Junior children could act out and retell a whole story themselves. You might let them use your puppets to repeat a story. Or ask a pupil to retell a story using your models.

DOING HANDWORK

There are many ways children can make things that relate to the story. But because of space and time limitations in the classroom, making pictures is the most widely used handwork activity.

Making a picture of something in the story is a very important part of the lesson for a child. Children express themselves in the pictures they make. Below is a variety of ways children can make pictures in class. The younger the children, the more you will need to prepare for them in advance, as well as help them in the classroom. But older children will enjoy making these pictures all by themselves.

For methods 2, 3, and 6 you will need pictures from your picture files.

1. **Drawing and Coloring**

    Let the child draw and color a complete picture of something he found meaningful in the story.

2. **Pasting on Part of the Picture**

    Let the child paste part of a picture onto a prepared background. Let the part pasted on be something of significance in the story.

    Example: "The Crucifixion" (Matt. 27; Mark 15; Luke 23; John 18:28-40 and chap. 19): Give each child a picture of a hill. Let him paste three crosses in place on the picture.

3. **Making a Montage**

    Paste part of a colored picture onto a plain sheet of paper. Let the child complete the picture, matching the colors and lines.

    Example: "Noah and the Ark" (Gen. 6—8, and 9:1-18, 28, 29): Give each child part of an animal picture pasted on a sheet of paper. It might be the front or hind quarters, or just the head. Let the child finish the picture. (See illus. 1, on page 101.)

4. **Crayon Rubbing**

    This method is especially good for making pictures in which the same object is repeated several times. From stiff paper, cut a pattern or patterns for significant objects in the story. Older children can make their own patterns. Let each child make a picture, repeating the object as many times as is necessary. Instead of tracing around the pattern on top of the paper, however, have the child put the pattern under the paper and rub over it with crayon.

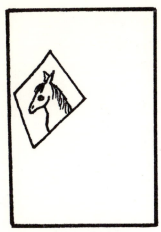  

ILLUSTRATION 1   ILLUSTRATION 2   ILLUSTRATION 3

Example: "Jesus Turns the Water to Wine" (John 2:1-12): Have the child make a picture of many water containers.

Example: "The Miracle of the Fishes" (Luke 5:1-11; John 21:6-14): Let each child make a net full of fishes.

5. **Making a Paper Mosaic Picture**

This project would not be suitable for preschool children. Have the child draw a simple scene from the story. Let him cut small tiles of colored paper and color the complete picture, leaving little lines of space around each tile. The child will need scissors to round off corners on some of the tiles. (See illus. 2.) You may need to prepare the tiles ahead of time. It would save time if you would put each color tile into a different little box. A good source of paper for this project is magazine pages on which there is a lot of solid color.

Example: "Jesus Calms the Storm" (Matt. 8:23-27; Mark 4:35-41; Luke 8:22-25): Have each child make a picture of a sailboat and fill it in with colored paper tiles.

6. **Assembling and Pasting a Puzzle**

Let each child paste a puzzle onto a sheet of paper. Make the puzzles up in advance. To make a puzzle, take a complete picture that represents the story or its meaning. Cut it into pieces. You will need to cut fewer pieces for smaller children. The pieces needn't be curved and complicated as in jigsaw puzzles. You might rather use an easier method, similar to that in illustration 3. Put each puzzle into an envelope. Give each child an envelope in class and let him reassemble and paste the puzzle onto a sheet of paper. If you trace around the puzzle picture on a sheet of paper before cutting the puzzle, the outline can serve as a guide when the child is reassembling and pasting the puzzle.

Example: "The Lord is My Shepherd" (Ps. 23): Make a puzzle for each child, using pictures of sheep from your picture files.

When a child finishes his picture, print or let him print the memory verse on it. Let older children make notebooks of their pictures and take them home at the end of the unit. Smaller children will want to take their pictures home each week. However, you might encourage their parents to paste the pictures into a booklet, or keep them in a folder for their children at home. Otherwise, loose pictures are usually thrown away, instead of serving as a good review at home.

If you have space in your classroom, you might display the pictures your children make. You can either put up all the pictures from week to week, or you could select one picture each week and mount it. At the end of the unit you would have one picture up for each story you have studied. If you do this, it would be good to give a different child a turn each week. If you have more than thirteen children in your class, you might need to put up more than one picture each week to be sure each child has a picture displayed during a unit.

Children could make pictures about many Bible stories, using these six methods we have outlined above. You will also learn many other ways as you continue teaching.

7. **Cardboard Puzzles**

Before we leave this chapter, here are some additional ideas for making and using cardboard puzzles. These puzzles are sturdy and can be used over and over again. Instructions are also given for making puzzle trays. Because the puzzle pieces are not interlocking, trays are necessary to hold them in place while the puzzle is being assembled. Making puzzles like these is an excellent way to utilize Bible pictures you may have. You might also experiment with other pictures that could be used for application of Bible stories.

Materials Needed

Corrugated cardboard
All purpose glue (ordinary paper glue is not satisfactory)
Linoleum cutter or similar sharp blade with a handle
Ruler
Wooden board or other surface on which you can cut
Colored pictures

How to Make Them

(1) Select a picture you wish to make into a puzzle.

(2) Cut two sheets of corrugated cardboard for the tray, about 2" wider than the picture on all sides.

(3) In the center of one sheet, trace around the picture.

(4) Cut out the rectangle you have traced.

(5) Put glue on the back of the remaining "frame" and paste it to the solid sheet. Set it under something heavy until the glue is dry.

(6) Paste the picture onto the cardboard center you have cut out. Be sure to spread the glue thinly on the entire surface of the picture back. Set it under something heavy until the glue dries.

(7) Trim it slightly on all sides.

(8) Using a ruler and pencil, divide the picture into 10-12 pieces on the wrong side. Use the same style as seen in illustration 3 on page 101.

(9) Cut out the pieces, going slightly past the end of each line to finish the corners neatly.

(10) If the first cut isn't quite deep enough, turn the puzzle face up and follow the perforated line from the top.

(11) Assemble the pieces in the cardboard tray for storing and handling.

Some Suggested Uses

(1) Presession Activity
Have cardboard puzzles and frames handy and give one to each child who comes to class early. Let him tell you the main points of the story represented in the picture he assembles.

(2) Review
If you have a puzzle for each story in a unit, give each child a puzzle and let him assemble it and tell the story for review at the end of the unit.

(3) Story Introduction
Have the children gather around the table and help you assemble the picture. Then hold it up and use it to introduce the story.

(4) Story Telling
  (a) Starting in the bottom left-hand corner and working in rows from left to right, number the puzzle pieces on the wrong side.

  (b) Write out the story, dividing it into as many parts as you have puzzle pieces.

  (c) Tell the story, putting up the puzzle piece that corresponds to each section.

  (d) When the story is complete, the children can see the picture that depicts it.

IMPORTANT: Teaching time is precious. Use it to teach!

10

HELPING CHILDREN APPLY THE PRINCIPLES OF BIBLE STORIES

WHAT IS APPLICATION?

If you have a broken vase and a tube of glue, how can you fix the vase? You will need to do something, won't you? You will have to put the glue where it is needed and stick the vase back together again. This is application. The tube of glue, although good in itself, will not fix the vase unless it is applied to the broken areas.

On the same principle, a head full of knowledge of Bible facts alone will not guarantee that a person will live the abundant life Christ promised His followers. This knowledge must be used when it is learned. The apostle James put it this way: "Only be sure that you act on the message and do not merely listen" (2:23, NEB). He goes on to say that the man who does the things he learns from God's Word will find happiness.

When children learn arithmetic, they are taught to use this knowledge to begin solving mathematical problems. For example, a child learns to use division to share a quantity of candy with a group of his friends. By working with problems like these, children gradually become prepared to solve the financial and mathematical problems they encounter as adults. Let's see how children can use Bible knowledge in the same practical way, taking the principles and using them in their everyday experiences. Then when they become adults they will continue to use these principles to build sound Christian lives.

WHAT ACTION SHOULD RESULT FROM BIBLE TEACHING?

Scripture was written to adults that they might develop the attitudes and behavior that would enable them to live happily now and eternally. One action is inward, the other outward. Correct thinking and doing are inseparable. Solomon said, As a man thinketh in his heart, so is he (Prov. 23:7). Our objective as teachers is to help children develop good thinking (also called attitudes) and good behavior. To help you in reaching this objective, we will examine the basic attitudes and behavior patterns a child needs to learn.

1. **Teach a child to love and trust God and he will let God direct him.**

We can help a child do this by emphasizing in our teaching that God made us, loves us dearly, and understands everything we need in order to be truly happy. When children learn how much God loves them, they will love God in return (I John 4:19). Children need to know much about God's love and concern for the human beings He created.

Many times adults as well as children do not understand why God gives us the instructions for living that He does. They are not for God's benefit, *they are for ours!* For example, Jesus said, "The sabbath was made for man, and not man for the sabbath" (Mark 2:27). By creating a day of rest and worship for people, God was answering two of man's needs—the need to worship and the need to rest from work. We can build children's confidence in God by showing them the joys that come to them, even as children, when they do the things God tells them. In the same way, we can show them the sad consequences of refusing to listen to Him. We hurt ourselves and others when we don't follow God's ways.

Obedience to God includes obedience to those God has given authority to: Christ, our parents, our teacher, the government, and so forth. However, God and Christ are the only infallible authorities. When men teach us to do anything that is against God's teachings, we must obey God rather than man.

2. **Teach a child to love others and he will do good to them.**

Why should children love and do good to others? In the first place, they are precious to God. He wants all the people of the earth to be in His family and be happy. Since we are God's children, we want to act like our Father would toward others.

Second, loving brings happiness. By being kind, patient, forgiving, friendly, generous, and thoughtful, we help make other people happy. When we make others happy, we find happiness ourselves.

Third, when we love and do good to others, we establish good relationships with them, which is life's most precious blessing.

3. **Teach a child to accept himself and he will have a healthy self-love.**

The offices of psychologists are overflowing with adults who learned as children to reject themselves. A child must know he has been created in God's beautiful image. By teaching a child that he is loved, despite his inability to do right all the time, you will help him accept himself and be patient with himself as he strives to do what is good.

To sum up what we are trying to get children to do as they learn God's Word, remember these words of Jesus: " 'Love the Lord your God with all your heart, with all your soul, with all your mind,' That is the greatest commandment. It comes first. The second is like it: 'Love your neighbour as yourself.' Everything in the Law and the prophets hangs on these two commandments" (Matt. 22:37-40, NEB).

HOW CAN WE HELP CHILDREN UNDERSTAND HOW THEIR ATTITUDES AND BEHAVIOR ARE TO BE AFFECTED?

You can help children understand by using modern stories, illustrations, and poems written on their level. Often it is sufficient to discuss the main point of the Bible story, giving examples of similar situations from the lives of children today. We will now elaborate on using application stories and illustrations.

APPLICATION STORIES

After teaching a historical Bible story, stress the moral, which we have defined as a good or bad way to behave or think. Then you might tell a short non-Biblical children's story with animal or children characters, who are acting like the characters in the Bible story. Be sure the children understand that this story is not from the Bible, but that it can help them better understand the lesson they can learn from the Bible story. Children identify with the characters in these stories. Two examples are "Peter Rabbit," which stresses the importance of obedience to parents, and "The Grasshopper and the Ants," which shows the importance of hard work and preparation. Young children enjoy animal stories. Older children like stories about children their own age or heroes of today.

AN APPLICATION STORY TO PREPARE WITH PICTURES

In addition to using stories like those above, you can make up your own stories. Below is one about a little girl who was never satisfied with what she had. She was very unhappy because of this bad attitude. You could use this story to show what it means to covet, when telling the story of Ahab taking Naboth's vineyard.

If you like, use visual aids when you make up a story. For "Discontent Dora" you might make a flip chart. After the title page, show a picture of an unhappy little girl with thought bubbles rising above her head, similar to a comic strip picture of someone thinking. For each point in the story, show a picture. When you get to the last point, turn back to the first picture of Dora. You will need to show Dora's picture twice when telling the story.

Discontent Dora

1. This is discontent Dora. Does she look like a happy little girl? No, she is very unhappy because she always wishes things were different. . . . She wishes she could look different.
2. "I hate brown hair! Why can't I have red hair like Sally?" she asks herself.
3. "I wish I could be thin like Jimmy," she thinks.
4. "If only I were taller, I would be so happy."
5. Discontent Dora isn't satisfied with anything she has. . . . She wishes she could have a baby sister instead of her little brother.
6. "If only I had lots of money," she wishes to herself.
7. "We'd have a beautiful new house."
8. "And a shiny red car instead of Daddy's old blue one."
9. "And I'd have a bicycle nicer than Tommy's."
10. Dora wishes she could have everything her way. . . . She thinks how nice it would be if she never had to practice her music lessons.

11. Or go to school.

12. Or brush her teeth.

13. "And why does it always have to rain?" she complains to herself.

14. Dora is always cross if anyone does anything better than she. She wishes she could be the fastest runner in the whole school.

15. Discontent Dora even wishes the time would move faster so she could have all the things she wants sooner. Will this make Dora happy?

16. No, Discontent Dora will never be happy until she learns a very important lesson from the Bible. The apostle Paul says, "I have learned to be satisfied with what I have" (Phil. 4:11). Are you happy?

ILLUSTRATIONS

In chapter 1 we pointed out that doctrinal passages are those which give instructions for living the Christian life, or symbolical descriptions to show the Christian's relationship with spiritual things. When showing children how doctrinal instructions apply to them, you might use the same type of story as those mentioned above. Or if the passage is a description, by using a physical thing to illustrate a spiritual one, you might explain to the children what the physical thing is like or how it behaves. This will help them understand the point. Some of the concepts you can explain in this way are: "The Lord Is My Shepherd," "The Church Is the Body of Christ," "A Christian Is a Royal Priest," "God's Word Is an Armor for the Christian," "Teaching the Gospel Is Like Sowing Seeds," "Christians Are the Salt of the Earth," and so forth.

AN ILLUSTRATION TO PREPARE FOR THE FLANNELBOARD

Below is a humorous illustration you could use when teaching the story "The Parable of the Fish Net" in chapter 5. By comparing the various fish to human beings, children can see examples of their own good or bad behavior. When you use this illustration, put each fish on the flannelboard as you talk about it.

Open Up the Fish Net

Here is a net full of fish. [Put the fish into the net you made for chapter 5 and hold it up.] Let's look at the fish inside and see if people don't sometimes act just like these fish!

1. **The Catfish.** If you look for a catfish in a fish tank or in the ocean, you will likely find him digging around in the dirt. He's always digging up rubbish. Some people spend all their time stirring up trouble, but the apostle Peter says we are not to be busybodies and troublemakers (I Peter 4:14).

2. **The Grunt Fish.** This is an unusual fish that goes around all day making funny grunting noises. Do you know any people who spend all their time grumbling and complaining?

3. **The Puffer** or **Balloon Fish.** You can see from this fish that he is full of air. Some people are like that—all puffed up with their own importance. They are too proud. The apostle Paul says we are to be humble, not puffed up (I Cor. 13:4).

4. **The Sailfish.** It would be nice to have a sail and glide along through life like a sailfish through water. But Jesus says we must take up our cross and follow Him (Matt. 16:24). Life isn't all smooth sailing.

5. **The Octopus.** What can we learn from this funny creature? Does anyone like to have a little octopus crawl on him? No! The octopus has long sticky feelers that he wraps around things. He also squirts out a cloud of inky fluid that keeps him hidden. Does this remind you of anyone? The devil is something like an octopus. So are those who do the devil's will. They hide their real selves and trick us into believing them.

6. **The Sucker.** We can guess from this fish's name what's wrong with him. A sucker is very easy to catch because it bites at anything. In I John 4:1 we are told to try every spirit and make sure it comes from God. We must read our Bibles carefully, so that false teachers don't trick us into believing them.

7. **The Jellyfish.** There are many unpleasant things about a jellyfish. But worst of all is that he has no backbone. He just moves to and fro. A Christian who lets himself be pulled away from serving God is acting just like a jellyfish.

8. **The Cod.** Have you ever had to take cod liver oil? Mothers give it to their children to keep them healthy. People who give their lives for good things are like this codfish.

9. **The Tuna Fish.** The tuna and many other kinds of fish are good to eat. God wants us to be good and useful.

10. **The Salmon.** If all people were like this fish it would be wonderful! The salmon is very eager to do her work. When it is time to lay her eggs, no matter where she is, she goes back home to the place

where she was born. It is very difficult to get there. The water is full of currents and she must swim against them. After she reaches her goal and lays her eggs, she is ready to die, happy and content that she has finished doing what she was made for. The apostle Paul said he had fought hard in his life to do what was right, and he knew that he was going to go to heaven when he died (II Tim. 4:8).

We want to be like the cod and tuna and salmon in our fish net. Then God will gather us up to Him in heaven when this life on earth is finished.

AN APPLICATION POEM TO PREPARE WITH PICTURES

To help younger children appreciate God's power and wisdom as seen in creation, here is a poem you might illustrate with pictures. Suggestions are given in the brackets. This illustrated poem might be used as a lesson in itself, following a reference to the creation of all living creatures in the Genesis account.

Our Great Creator

Let's go off through nature land.
I wonder what we'll see.
I want to see the animals
God made for you and me. [*picture of a child observing an animal or another creature*]

We read about them in His Word,
How each of them He made,
How Adam gave them all their names
And with them often played. [*pic of this part of creation*]
God made the lovely colors
Of the lizard [*pic*] and the moth [*pic*]
And painted rainbows on the fish
Like patterns on a cloth. [*pic of striped fish*]
He gave the leopard inky spots, [*pic*]
The zebra stripes of black and white, [*pic*]
He sprayed the feathers of the birds
With colors, oh, so very bright! [*pic of colorful birds*]

Thank you, God, for the beautiful creatures you have made.

There's the bleating lamb God made.
He isn't very big. [*pic*]
Hear the bawling little calf [*pic*]
And squealing baby pig. [*pic*]

God made the geese's noisy honk, [*pic*]
The lion's fearful roar [*pic*]
And gave the puppies yelps and barks, [*pic of puppies*]
And other sounds to many more.

Thank you, God, for the sounds the animals make.

The animals move gracefully.
Just watch them as they go!
The birds float softly through the air, [*pic*]
The shiny fish glide to and fro. [*pic*]
The rabbit skips and hops along.
Down the path he goes. [*pic*]
The gentle deer springs from the ground
And nimbly comes down on his toes. [*pic*]

Thank you, God, for the graceful movement of the animals.

Now we've found some animals
Most interesting to see.
The opossom babies cling to her
As mother climbs a tree. [*pic*]
The elephant has such a trunk,
It reaches to the ground.
He uses it to work, and drink
Where water can be found. [*pic of an elephant*]
The tall giraffe has neck so long
It stretches to the sky.
He eats the top leaves from the trees
And watches birds fly by. [*pic of giraffe*]
The kangaroo can hop quite far
And box things with her paws and feet.
Her baby peeks out from his pouch.
Don't you think he's sweet? [*pic of kangaroo with baby in her pouch*]

Thank you, God, for the animals that are interesting to watch.

Some animals God gave for pets
To be our little friends.
The puppies [*pic*] and the kittens [*pic*]
Bring us joy that never ends.

Thank you, God, for our pets.

Some animals have strong, firm backs
To pull or carry heavy loads.
Watch the camel, [*pic*] horse, [*pic*] and donkey [*pic*]
As they go along the roads.

Some animals God gives for food
To help us grow up strong and tall. [*pic of a table set for a meal*]
Just think how awful it would be
If there weren't any meat at all! [*pic of meat assortment*]
God gives us beef and chicken, [*pic*]
Good fish and mutton stew. [*pic*]
From porky pigs He gives us ham
And it's delicious too! [*pic of a ham*]
The helpful cow gives more than meat: [*pic of cow*]
She gives us yellow cheese to eat, [*pic*]
Fresh milk, [*pic*] and butter for our bread, [*pic*]
And ice cream for a special treat. [*pic*]
And leather comes from cows, you know,
For purses, shoes, and other things. [*pic of these items*]
On leather scrolls men wrote God's Word,
Which to mankind salvation brings. [*pic of scroll and Bible*]
The sheep is such a useful friend, [*pic*]
He gives us balls of wool so fine [*pic*]
To make so many kinds of clothes
To keep us warm in wintertime. [*pic of clothes from catalog*]
God gives us eggs from chickens,
They're nice cooked any way. [*pic of eggs*]
Some pillows are with feathers stuffed
For sleepy heads at close of day. [*pic*]

Thank you, God, for useful animals that help us in so many ways.

For creatures that we see and hear,
We thank you, Lord, today.
We're glad you made them as you did
In your own special way. [*pic of a child praying or one observing one of God's creatures*]

HOW CAN WE MOTIVATE CHILDREN TO DO WHAT THEY LEARN?

If we use effective teaching principles and methods like those we have learned in this course, children will develop a sound faith in God and a conscience that can see the difference between right and wrong. Thus, good teaching will automatically result in these aspects of a child's inner development. When there is a principle in a Bible story that can be applied to a child's outer behavior, you can motivate him to respond in some of the following ways:

1. **Singing.** When children sing songs like the second type we mentioned in chapter 9, they express verbally their desire to do what they have learned.

2. **Praying.** After teaching them what action is necessary, let the children talk to God about it. Teach children to give thanks to God for the way He blesses them, and to ask for His help in doing what is right.

   It is good to let the children take turns praying. Sometimes you might have all the children pray during prayer time. Let each say a sentence after you have discussed things we are thankful for, or something we need God's help to do.

3. **Experimenting and Discussing.** Encourage the children to try outside the classroom the things they learn in class. Then give them opportunity to discuss the results. For example, if you are studying the miracles of Jesus, help children learn to be compassionate toward others as Jesus was. Suggest that they try that week to do something good for someone who is elderly, sick, or handicapped. Let them talk about what they did the following week. In this way they will learn the happiness we experience when we do good things for others, as the Bible teaches us to do.

   Also, when studying behavior patterns to avoid, give the children opportunity to tell about something they suffered because they failed to do what they should have.

4. **Class Projects.** Class projects like the ones below help children learn to practice together the most essential action of Christianity—that of helping others. Some good projects for this purpose are:

   a. Inviting others to learn the Bible with us. (See attendance booster charts on p. 88.)

   b. Bringing clothing or food items to class for those who are in need.

   c. Collecting money in class for an object to give to a missionary or someone in need.

d. Writing cards to members of the congregation that are ill or shut in. You might keep a box of cards in your classroom. Let all the children who can write sign it, or you sign it for each of the little children.

Helping children apply the principles of Scripture seems like a lot of hard work. If you will collect appropriate stories, poems, and songs as you run across them, filing them away carefully, you will find the job much easier.

Having a definite purpose with each Bible story you teach will also help. Decide by the contents of the passage how you can use it to build up faith or develop good attitudes and behavior. Always encourage the children to try God's ways.

SUGGESTIONS FOR FILING APPLICATION STORIES AND ILLUSTRATIONS

1. Prepare three file folders for application stories. (Include illustrations like the one in this chapter, too.) Notice the file headings suggested in Section III on page 128.

2. On the top right corner of each application story or illustration, write the attitude or behavior it pertains to.

3. File all the stories in alphabetical order according to their titles.

It is very difficult to file these stories and illustrations any other way. If you file the application story with a Bible story it can be used in conjunction with, you won't be able to find it if you want to use it with another story that teaches the same lesson. If you try to make separate folders for each attitude and behavior pattern, you will find much overlapping.

PART FOUR

AN ORGANIZED TEACHER

11

LESSON PLANS

Now that you have learned the fundamentals of preparing and presenting Bible stories to children, let us spend some time learning how to write up plans for complete units and lessons. These plans will include what you want to teach, how you plan to teach it, and what materials you will need.

Teaching from lesson plans pays great dividends. Notice a few of these:

1. You, as a teacher, will have much more confidence that things will go smoothly. And they will!

2. The children will learn the maximum amount you are able to teach them in a class period.

3. Discipline problems will be at a minimum.
4. You will have everything prepared for your lesson and nothing will be forgotten as your class period proceeds.
5. You will be ready to reteach a unit any time you need to.

Here are two outlines for lesson plans—one for the unit plan and one for individual lesson plans. Refer to your card file when you are making up these plans.

THE UNIT PLAN

Select thirteen stories based on a period of history, a subject, or a moral. If you are using a quarterly, these stories will already be selected for you. Prepare a Unit Plan sheet.

Your aim for the unit will be to teach and apply the theme of the unit. If it is a historical unit, your aim will be to show how God worked among the people in that particular period of history, and to learn lessons from the lives of the characters who lived at that time.

List the titles of the stories. Write down the materials you will need for your theme bulletin board and attendance charts.

Here is a sample Unit Plan sheet.

UNIT PLAN

Title:

Aim:

Grade or Age Level:

Dates: From   to

LESSONS INCLUDED:

1.
2.
3.
4.
5.
6.
7.
8.
9.
10.
11.
12.
13.

MATERIALS NEEDED FOR ROOM DECORATIONS:

Bulletin Board:

1.
2.
3.
4.
5.

Attendance Charts:

1.
2.
3.
4.

MATERIALS NEEDED FOR CLASS PROJECT:

1.
2.

THE LESSON PLAN

Prepare a lesson plan sheet for each story in the unit. Your aim for each lesson will be to teach and apply the moral or subject of each story.

The memory verse could be the key verse or portion of a verse that expresses the main point of the story, or a verse from any part of the Bible that states the lesson the story has in view.

List specific visual aids you will need for teaching the story, such as which puppet characters you will need, the illustrated application story you are going to use, and so forth.

If you are using a quarterly, just write "See page ___" under the section on your sheet marked "Questions."

The time schedule given on the next page is just an example of how you might divide up the time in a one-hour class period. The order of events is up to you. Also, the amount of time you devote to each part of the lesson will vary from week to week.

Under "Evaluation" at the end of each lesson plan, write down a brief note on how the lesson went and what you might do to improve it next time.

Here is a sample Lesson Plan sheet.

LESSON PLAN

Unit Title:

Story Title:

Aim:

Date:

Scripture:

Memory Verse:

Methods:

Visual Aids Needed:

1.
2.
3.
4.

Handwork Activity:

Materials Needed:

1.
2.
3.
4.

Songs:

1.
2.

Questions:

1.
2.
3.
4.
5.

Time Schedule:

7:00 - 7:10   Opening prayer; mark attendance charts; memory verses
7:10 - 7:15   Review
7:15 - 7:30   Today's story
7:30 - 7:35   Song; questions
7:35 - 7:45   Application
7:45 - 8:00   Handwork; closing prayer

Evaluation:

When you plan to tell a story with models or puppets, you might add one more section to your lesson plan entitled *Story Outline.* List the scenes or manipulations in this section.

SUGGESTIONS FOR FILING WRITTEN PLANS

1. When you have prepared and taught a complete unit, clip or staple all the plan sheets together, including the bulletin board sketch.
2. File them in the folder marked "Lesson Plans and Quarterlies."

A SAMPLE LESSON TO STUDY

The sample lesson that follows could be used as part of a unit for primary children, based on the theme "Greed" or "Covetousness."

The numbers in brackets behind several parts of the lesson plan refer you back to the pages of this book that deal with these items.

LESSON PLAN NO. 5

Unit Title: "Thou Shalt Not Covet"

Story Title: "Naboth's Vineyard

Aim: To show the children how covetousness can lead a person to do things for which he will be sorry later.

Date: January 28, 1973

Scripture: I Kings 21:1-20

Memory Verse: "Then they took him outside the city and stoned him, and sent word to Jezebel that Naboth had been stoned to death" (I Kings 21:14, NEB).

Methods: Word Picture Story; Application Picture Story

Visual Aids Needed:

1. Grapevine and grapes [pp. 52-53]
2. Flannelboard and stand [p. 43]
3. Application Picture Story, "Discontent Dora" [pp. 108-109]

Handwork Activity: Montage [p. 100]

Materials Needed:

1. Pictures of grape clusters
2. Scissors
3. Paper
4. Glue
5. Crayons

Songs:

1. "Count Your Blessings" (chorus only)

Questions: (Fill in the Blanks)

1. _____ and _____ were the king and queen of Israel.
2. Ahab wanted a vineyard that belonged to _____.
3. Ahab tried to _____ the vineyard, but Naboth would not sell it.
4. When _____ found out about the problem, she promised to get the vineyard for Ahab.
5. She wrote a _____, saying that Naboth must be
6. When Naboth was dead, Ahab _____ the vineyard for his own.
7. But God was very _____.
8. The prophet _____ came to tell Ahab and Jezebel they would die terrible deaths because of their wickedness.

Time Schedule:

7:00 — 7:10 Opening Prayer
             Mark attendance charts
             Memory verse (last week's if one was assigned)
7:10 — 7:15 Review questions over last week's lesson
7:15 — 7:30 Today's story
7:30 — 7:35 Questions over today's lesson
7:35 — 7:45 Application story "Discontent Dora"
             Application song "Count Your Blessings"
7:45 — 8:00 Handwork
             Closing prayer

Evaluation: The memory verse was a little too long for primary students. Next time use the first part of Exodus 20:17 as the memory verse. The children especially enjoyed the application story.

12

FILING TEACHING MATERIALS

A good filing system can be a great asset to a teacher. Likewise, the failure to have one is a great liability. Look at these advantages of a filing system:

1. Everything is easy to find when you need it.
2. Your teaching materials last longer when they are carefully put away.
3. Organized material takes up less space in your home.

It is well worth your while to prepare a good expandable filing system early in your career as a teacher.

MATERIALS YOU WILL NEED

About 60 legal-size file folders (14" x 9½")
5 filing dividers
A cardboard box in which you can stand your files

Labeled Boxes

If you have been following the filing suggestions throughout the course, you should have labeled boxes containing the following:

Bible Story Card File
Work Tools
Puppets
Models

Continue to file bulky material in this way. You might ask someone to make you a large flat box in which you can put flat materials that are too large to be filed in regular file folders. Have it made large enough to hold your flannelboard and easel, posters, charts, large items from bulletin board displays, and so forth.

File Folders

Below is a filing system that will hold any flat materials that can be fitted into file folders.

In the first section, file any materials you study about the Bible, or teaching principles. There is also a place in this section for your lesson plans.

In Section III, file all materials from which you can draw to make up Bible lessons.

In Sections IV and V, file flat Bible stories you have prepared, such as flip charts and flannelgraph stories. The stories you illustrated for chapters 4 and 5 are listed already. Remember that puppet and model stories are to be recorded in your card file.

SECTION I: TEACHER'S PREPARATION

Bible Study Notes
Lesson Plans and Quarterlies
Teaching Preschoolers
Teaching Primaries
Teaching Juniors

SECTION II: LESSON PREPARATION MATERIALS—PICTURES

Animals
Behavior—Bad
Behavior—Good
Body Parts
Children
Fish
Food
Foreign People and Places
The Home
Insects

Miscellaneous
Objects
Occupations
People with Problems
Plants
Religious Pictures
Scenery
School
Weather
Worship

SECTION III: LESSON PREPARATION MATERIALS—GENERAL

Application Stories (a-h)
Application Stories (i-o)
Application Stories (p-z)
Bulletin Board Sketches
Attendance Chart Ideas
Handwork Ideas
Illustrated Memory Verses - O.T.

Illustrated Memory Verses - N.T.
Letters
Storytelling Ideas
Patterns
Poems
Songs

SECTION IV: PREPARED STORIES—OLD TESTAMENT

Manufactured Flannelgraph Stories — O.T.
Naboth's Vineyard (I Kings 21:1-20)

SECTION V: PREPARED STORIES—NEW TESTAMENT

Manufactured Flannelgraph Stories — N.T.
The Parable of the Fish Net (Matt. 13:47-50)
The Prodigal Son (Luke 15:11-32)
What Is Heaven Like? (Rev. 21)

ILLUSTRATION 4

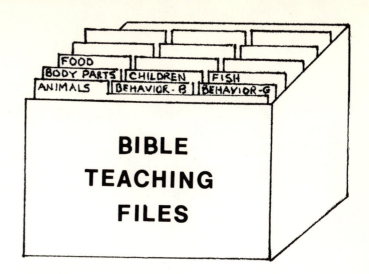

HOW TO PREPARE AND ARRANGE FILE FOLDERS

You will notice that your file folders are made so that the little tabs on the top of the folders are cut in different positions. In order to read all the headings on the folders when they are in your file box, you will need to arrange the file folders in each section. If your folders have three different tab positions, the first folder will be a left tab, the second a center tab, the third a right tab, the fourth a left tab, and so on in this order throughout the section. (See illus. 4.) As you expand your system later, try not to put two folders with the same tab position directly behind one another.

With a thin black marker, print the headings on the tabs after the folders are all in order. Or type these headings. You will need to abbreviate words that are too long.

HOW TO MAKE DIVIDERS

To make a divider for each section, trace a center tab folder onto a heavy sheet of colored paper. Cut it out and print the section heading on it. It is not necessary to print the word *Section* or the number on the divider.

HOW TO EXPAND THIS SYSTEM

With a filing system like this, you are basically organized for the rest of your career. You will find it necessary from time to time to add folders for additional topics. However, they should fit into one of the sections you already have. If not, just prepare another section divider.

When a folder becomes too full, split the material up into several folders. For example, if your "Animals" folder is overcrowded, make two new folders. Label the original one "Animals—Farm"; the second, "Animals—General"; and the third, "Animals—Pets."

You may need to add another box for your files. Just leave the first two or three sections in the original box and move the others to the new box. Eventually, you may need a filing cabinet!

13

A TEACHER'S
TOTAL PREPARATION

In this final chapter, we will sum up all the things we have studied in this course. The chapter will also serve as somewhat of a procedure you might follow in your teaching activities.

CONTINUE YOUR TEACHER-TRAINING PROGRAM

Learn all you can from the sermons you hear and the Bible study classes you attend. All the additional knowledge you gain from now on will help you to be a better teacher.

Study the characteristics, needs, and abilities of children in the different age groups, especially the group you are teaching.

Keep up with the latest developments in teaching techniques. Here are some ways you might do this:

1. Attend teachers' workshops.
2. Visit the classrooms of other teachers.
3. Read teaching books and magazines.
4. Look through religious catalogs periodically.

BUILD UP YOUR TEACHING RESOURCES

Resources are materials like those listed in Sections II and III of the suggested filing system. The more good materials you have in these files, the less searching you will need to do as you prepare for each lesson.

Teachers' workshops usually provide a wealth of ideas in the areas of storytelling, bulletin board displays, new songs, and so forth. When you attend a workshop, copy down these ideas and file them away until you need them.

PLAN AND PREPARE FOR UNITS OF STUDY IN ADVANCE

Keeping in mind our overall aim as teachers, select a moral, subject, or period of history you can use as a theme for a unit. Remember, we are trying to help each child develop good attitudes and behavior toward God, himself, and others. Have a goal in mind as you teach each unit.

Plan the Unit

1. Using your card file, select thirteen stories that bear out the theme you have chosen. (You may want to use less than thirteen stories at times.)
2. Plan a theme bulletin board and attendance charts, and a class project that is related to the main idea of the unit or the general theme of Christianity.
3. Write down all the necessary information on a Unit Plan sheet.
4. Prepare any materials you will need for the room decorations and the class project.

Plan Each Lesson

1. Begin early in each week to make your plans.
2. Prepare a Lesson Plan sheet.

3. Write down all the information that pertains to the story, application, and class activities you intend to use.

4. Study the story carefully.

5. Know it well enough to tell it if you are going to be using models, puppets, or flannelgraph figures.

6. Prepare your visual aids for the whole lesson.

7. Practice using any visualized material you are going to present to the class.

WHEN YOU ARE USING QUARTERLY UNITS MAKE THEM YOUR OWN

If a preacher was to stand up each week and read someone else's sermon outlines exactly as they were written, we would soon become bored with his preaching. In the same way, children become restless when their teacher depends too much on the quarterly from which she is teaching. This need never happen.

Quarterlies vary in the amount of teaching material they provide. However, most of them contain a unit outline and lesson plans which include the story in appropriate language, the memory verse, questions, some type of application, song suggestions, and handwork activity.

If you will glance back over the list of points we have just given, you will see that using quarterlies cuts a teacher's work down by at least half. But don't neglect the other half! Before the unit begins, look through the whole teacher's manual and student's workbook. Then make your Unit and Lesson Plans just as you would if you were making up the lessons completely by yourself.

If you are using quarterlies, you will have more time to prepare visual aids. Don't just read the story from the quarterly or the Bible week after week. Try to visualize Bible stories for the children as often as possible, even for juniors. It may seem like a great deal of work to prepare visual aids for each story; but after you have used the story in the unit for which you have prepared it, you can use it again and again with your own children or in other units.

Most of the types of story-telling visual aids we have discussed in this course can be used with children in any age group. You just need to adjust the language according to the age of the children in the class. Therefore, if you prepare dozens of visualized stories over the weeks and months ahead, you will always be ready to take on new teaching challenges in any age group.

When you have the time, visualize some of the other parts of the quarterly lesson, such as the memory verse, new songs, application stories, and so forth. And do try to prepare bulletin board displays and attendance charts that relate to the quarterly units.

Instead of using the same type of quarterly picture as a handwork activity every week, try some of the suggestions from chapter 10. You could even combine some of these ideas with the handwork the quarterly gives.

Teaching with quarterlies can be just as exciting and challenging as teaching from units you completely prepare yourself. Whichever way you teach, be an individual. Put yourself into what you are teaching.

This course has come to an end, but you are really just beginning. Ask God to help you daily in this great and wonderful work you have undertaken!

SOME SUGGESTIONS FOR CONDUCTING A TEACHERS' TRAINING CLASS

If you are an experienced teacher and would like to train others to teach, this book can provide the foundation for your class. Although the organization and presentation of the course will vary from one congregation to another, here are some suggestions for you to consider.

Organizing the Class

1. If there is an educational director in your congregation, you will need to discuss the class with him. Let him know how you intend to teach it. Decide what materials the church will be able to provide and what materials the students will need to provide. When you begin teaching, be sure to show the students all of the materials which are available to them at the church building.

2. Recruit prospective teachers. There are probably a number of women and older teen-age girls in your congregation who could teach. You might also find a few men who would be interested. Approach each person individually, and tell her you think she would make a good teacher. Assure her that there is a great need for her services as a teacher. Let her know a training class is about to begin and invite her to come.

3. Call a meeting of all those who agree to take the course. Decide on the time of the week that suits them. You may need to have the class during one of the periods when the church is already meeting. Tell the students approximately how long the class will continue. To cover the whole course as we are going to suggest here, you will need to plan on meeting weekly for about six months.

4. Be sure to have a copy of the book for each student before you begin your first class.

Supplementing the Material in This Book

1. Add information from your own experience.

2. Incorporate ideas you have gained from other teachers' training literature.

3. Invite speakers to enlarge on some of the subjects you would like to see covered more fully.

4. Bring to class any manufactured materials you may have that relate to the various sections of the course.

5. If one is available, bring along a catalog of teaching materials the students can buy or order through the church.

6. If you have the opportunity, you might visit a teachers' workshop together as a class.

Encouraging the Students to Do Their Assignments

1. Be enthusiastic! If you are excited about effective teaching and the good results it can bring, you will inspire your students to be the same.

2. Try to do all of the assignments yourself. Then use plenty of expression when you present the example stories and class activities from the book, as well as those from your own files.

3. Have the students begin their card files as soon as you come to the instructions in the book. In order to cover the whole Bible while the class is in session, you might assign about six chapters of reading and note taking each day, instead of three. Remind the students that this is light reading, for the purpose of selecting teachable stories and seeing how each story fits into the Bible's overall structure. Have them bring their card files to class periodically so you can check them. If the students do not work on their card files consistently, they will lose much of their value toward the end of the course.

4. When you come to the last part of chapter 3, have the students make up their complete set of file folders as instructed in chapter 13. To help them get everything set up correctly, it would be a good idea to have them do their files together in class. You might buy the folders for the whole class, then have each student pay for her share. This would save the students from having to go to an office supply store individually. The folders would also be cheaper if bought by the box.

As soon as their file folders are complete, assign the students to collect at least fifty good pictures for their picture files.

5. Have the students work up all the example stories and visual aids in chapters 4, 5, 6, and 7 as soon as you come to them. Also, have them prepare one more story of their own choice, using each of the six methods again.

You might have them work up at least part of their basic set of models in class so they could share materials. To save them some time on their puppets, you might suggest that they ask others outside the class to help them.

6. When you are studying manufactured flannelgraph stories in chapter 5, try to demonstrate a sample story for the students.

7. If you are presenting all of the example stories from the book yourself, it wouldn't be necessary to have the students demonstrate the same ones. However, it would be good to have them present the stories they have prepared from their own ideas. This way, if you have ten students and each of them prepares six stories in addition to the six in the book, each student will receive ideas for preparing sixty-six visualized stories! Give the class enough time to take down the ideas in their notebooks as each story is presented.

   When the students prepare their model stories, they will likely invent some new models for the others to copy. For example, if a student decides to tell the story of the lost sheep, he might make a sheepfold from the sides of a shallow cardboard box covered with wallpaper that looks like stone.

   It might be a good idea to assign the students the stories they are to prepare. The information at the beginning of each chapter will help you decide which stories to assign for each method.

8. When you are discussing singing, you might have each student make up a song and sing it to the class with or without visual aids. Once again, give the students time to copy down the words and ideas. Or, you might have someone mimeograph the songs.

9. When you are studying visualized application stories, illustrations, and memory verses, have each student present an example.

10. When you come to the chapter on room decorations, prepare and mount a theme bulletin board-attendance chart display. You might use one of the ideas from the book, or one of your own creations. Seeing a complete mounted display will show the students how effective this can be.

11. When you are studying chapter 11, find out which age group each of the students would like to teach. If some of the students are not particular, suggest that they teach one of the age groups in which the others have shown the least interest. Then have each student make up a unit outline for the age group she has chosen, along with a theme bulletin board-attendance chart sketch and a complete lesson plan for one of the stories in the unit. Have her make the sketch large enough for the other students to see. Let her hold it

up and explain to the class how she intends to develop it. Check her Unit and Lesson Plans.

12. Instead of having each student present a complete lesson in class, you might present one yourself, as if the class were a group of children. Then arrange for each student to present her lesson to a class of children the age for which she has prepared it.

13. Give the class a written test over the whole course, according to the way you have conducted it.

Getting Newly Trained Teachers into the Educational Program of the Church

1. The last session the class meets, have the educational director come in and make a teaching schedule for the new teachers, according to the age group they have chosen. If the students are to teach from quarterlies, have him give them the ones they are to use for their first unit. If they are to make up their own units, have them complete the ones they outlined earlier and use them.

2. There are several ways new teachers might begin teaching in the classrooms at the church building. Two new teachers might prepare and teach their first unit together. Or a new teacher might work with an experienced teacher for one unit. If this is done, have the two teachers prepare and present alternate lessons throughout the unit, rather than having the new teacher act as an assistant. A third way a teacher might begin is by teaching alone. If she is to teach by herself from the beginning, a new teacher will likely need a little more encouragement from you than those who are teaching in pairs. The way teachers are placed for their first real teaching assignment will depend on the situation in your congregation. However, be sure to assign a class to each new teacher as soon as possible.

There are so many advantages to having a teachers' training class in your congregation. The greatest, perhaps, is having an abundance of well-trained Bible teachers. With enough teachers from which to choose, the educational director can make up a schedule whereby each teacher can teach three months, then have three months to prepare for her next unit and to attend an adult Bible class herself. Also, there will be enough teachers so that many of them can go out and teach in the communities of those who can't come to your church building.

You, as a teacher-trainer, can inspire many teachers to be a part of fulfilling our Lord's great commission.

CONCLUSION
YOUR FUTURE AS A TEACHER

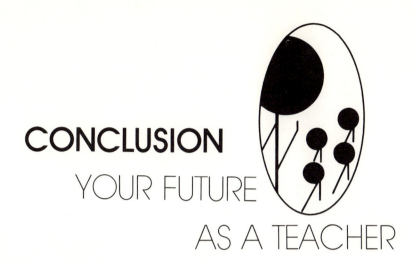

Now that you have completed a basic training course, where will you teach? There are several teaching possibilities for you to consider. If you are needed in the Bible school program at the church building, you will want to start there. Sunday is the most suitable day for Bible classes, and the church building is usually arranged with the equipment and furniture a teacher needs. However, it is not always practical or possible to get all of the children who need to be taught to the church building.

Therefore, we need teachers who will take their materials and teach in neighborhoods and institutions where children are not being taught. It would be a good idea for several teachers to work together in a "mission" effort like this. You would need to inquire as to what building or park may be available for classes, or which children's institutions in your city may require Bible teachers.

A third possibility is starting a class in your home for children in your neighborhood. If you have children of your own, let them help you recruit students.

Don't be afraid to knock on doors in your own neighborhood or around the church building, to invite parents to send their children to Bible classes. Tell them what type of program is planned for their children. Show them that you are interested and concerned. Why have only a few children in our Bible classes, when, with just a little effort, we could be teaching so many more!

Teaching the Bible to children has wonderful rewards for you and them. The greatest reward of all will be entering heaven one day and seeing others there that you have helped teach God's ways. May He bless you.

BIBLIOGRAPHY

Egermeier, Elsie E. *Egermeier's Bible Story Book*. Anderson, Ind.: The Warner Press, 1963.

Flynn, Leslie B. "Through the Bible in a Year" (tract). Oradell, New Jersey: American Tract Society, n.d.

Good News for Modern Man. New York: American Bible Society, 1966.

Mitchell, Evelyn. *Bible Story-Telling Puppets*. Cincinnati: Standard Publishing Company.

The New English Bible. Oxford: At the University Press, 1970.

Tilotta, Becky. *Your Handful of Ideas*. Austin, Tex.: Firm Foundation Publishing Co., n.d.